501 IDEAS FOR YOUR COMPLIANCE AND ETHICS PROGRAM

Lessons from 30 Years of Practice

JOSEPH E. MURPHY, JD, CCEP

Copyright © 2008 by the Society of Corporate Compliance & Ethics

Printed in the United States of America. All rights reserved. This book or parts thereof may not be reproduced in any form without the express written permission of the publisher.

ISBN 978-0-9792210-3-3

This publication is designed to provide accurate and authoritative information in regard to the subject matter covered. It is sold with the understanding that neither the author nor the publisher is engaged in rendering legal, accounting, or other professional service. If legal advice or other expert assistance is required, the services of a competent professional person should be sought (from a Declaration of Principles jointly adopted by a Committee of the American Bar Association and a Committee of Publishers).

To order copies of this publication, please contact:

Society of Corporate Compliance & Ethics
6500 Barrie Road, Suite 250
Minneapolis, MN 55435

Phone: +1 952 933 4977
Fax: +1 952 988 0146
Web site: www.corporatecompliance.org
e-mail: info@corporatecompliance.org

Contents

Foreword...V

What This Book Is About..VII

A. U.S. Organizational Sentencing Guidelines
   ("USSGs") Item 1, codes and policies............................ 1

B. USSGs Item 1, compliance controls................................ 9

C. USSGs item 2, compliance officer and infrastructure......... 11

D. USSGs item 2, the board and senior management........... 20

E. Winning management over... 27

F. USSGs item 3, background checks,
   diligence in hiring, and promotions............................ 31

G. USSGs item 4, training 34

H. USSGs item 4, other communications tools................. 43

I. USSGs item 5, helplines, reporting systems,
   preventing retaliation... 48

J. USSGs item 5, compliance audits 54

K. USSGs item 5, other types of checking systems,
   monitoring techniques, and program evaluations........ 57

L. USSGs item 6, discipline 63

M. USSGs item 6, incentives, rewards, recognition 66

N. USSGs item 7, responses and investigations 71

O. USSGs item c, risk assessment 77

P. Industry practices, benchmarking 81

Q. Third parties, joint ventures 84

R. Miscellaneous/other 88

S. Documentation 91

T. Antitrust and fair competitive practices compliance 93

U. FCPA/foreign corruption compliance 97

V. Consumer protection, sales practices,
    and advertising compliance 100

W. Gifts and conflicts of interest compliance 101

Bibliography of sources 103

Foreword

I first met Joe Murphy over a decade ago when we were chance seat partners on an airplane headed to one of the first compliance conferences in New Orleans. The two of us discussed many things on that flight but one lasting first impression has remained with me: Joe Murphy is a man of experience, intelligence, kindness, professionalism, and forethought. Through my many interactions and conversations with and about Joe, I am often reminded of a famous quotation, "If I have seen further, it is by standing on the shoulders of giants." This quote is often attributed to Sir Isaac Newton; however, its origins have an ancient history and meaning that predates Newton's use of the words.

The quotation embodies concepts regarding the transfer of human knowledge. Human knowledge and its understanding are a complex and cumulative affair. The passage of knowledge from those who have achieved it (as well as the wisdom associated with it) to those who have a need to learn is a hallmark of Joe Murphy's life. Joe's book, *501 Ideas for Your Compliance and Ethics Program*, embodies this ideal.

The conventional wisdom in this day and age is that the compliance and ethics profession is nascent. We are said to be members of a growth industry and members of an evolving professional group. As members of the new profession, we have an acute need to learn. The profession will likely change at a rapid pace, and our challenge as members of this new profession is to learn, master, and implement without error. Joe Murphy has given us an invaluable gift, a compilation of his thoughts and ideas based on his lifelong learning. We now have the duty to absorb it and pass it forward in the spirit in which it is given. Joe, thank you for this precious gift: you are a "giant" in both word and deed. Your foresight and generosity have permitted us to see further.

Odell Guyton
Co-chair, Society of Corporate
Compliance and Ethics (SCCE)
Advisory Board

What This Book Is About

Welcome to *501 Ideas for Your Compliance and Ethics Program*. If your job includes responsibility for any part of a compliance and ethics program, this book is meant for you. Whether you are only dealing with antitrust compliance in the U.S., or manage a comprehensive ethics and compliance program throughout the world, this book is designed to be your easy companion.

In this book I offer you a variety of ideas for your program. Perhaps you will be able to use hundreds of them, or maybe there will be just a few that meet some difficult challenges you are facing. Even better, maybe some of the ideas here will inspire you to come up with new ideas that drive your program to increased effectiveness. My goal here is to make your life as a compliance and ethics professional easier by giving you a handy source of ideas for your program.

I believe this will be especially valuable for those charged with the day-to-day task of making compliance and ethics a reality in their organizations. I should also explain what this book is not intended to do. It is not a treatise on the whys and wherefores of compliance; there are other good books on the market that do this well. It is definitely not a checklist of things every program has to do. The government and other sources already offer this kind of guidance, in such places as the U.S. Sentencing Commission's Organizational Guidelines and Australia's compliance program standards, AS 3806-2006. This book is also not intended to be a list of "best practices" that only gold standard companies embrace; for the most part, the items listed here are intended neither to be minimum standards for programs, nor a list of the requirements for top notch programs. It is not expected that any company would do everything in this book. Rather, the ideas listed here are intended as bite-sized nuggets to help compliance and ethics people do their jobs more effectively.

For the most part, I have omitted advocacy, analysis, and judgment from the list. If you, the reader, want to know in more detail why these ideas work or how to do them effectively, for most of the ideas I have provided source references for more background and detail. These are primarily sources I have worked with personally—materials I have written and articles from *ethikos*, which I co-edit. I leave it up to you to determine which steps you think will work in your company or organization.

This book does not offer legal advice or interpretation. For at least some of these ideas, you will want to consult with legal counsel who have compliance and ethics expertise. You will want to be sure any particular idea is legal in your jurisdiction, and determine whether there are restrictions such as those that may be found in privacy and labor laws.

I have included a variety of practical ideas, but I am certain there are many more great ideas out there waiting to be shared with others. If you have any you would like to share and have included in future editions of this book, please contact me at the e-mail address below. I would also like to hear of your experiences in trying any of these ideas, and perhaps include what you learned from trying them for the future guidance of others.

Joe Murphy, CCEP
jemurphy@voicenet.com

501 IDEAS FOR YOUR COMPLIANCE AND ETHICS PROGRAM

A. U.S. Organizational Sentencing Guidelines ("USSGs") Item 1, codes and policies

Ideas on compliance-related policies and on enhancing your code of conduct. These address part of USSGs item 1.

1 **Value statement.** Include compliance and ethics points in the company values statement, such as a commitment to integrity. This can also be incorporated into the company's mission statement. (See Sigler & Murphy, *Interactive Corporate Compliance: An Alternative to Regulatory Compulsion* (Westport, CT: Quorum Books, 1988): 82; Roach & Davis, "Establishing a Culture of Ethics and Integrity in Government," *ethikos* 21 no. 2 (Sept./Oct. 2007): 1, 3.)

2 **Index.** Include an index in the code, so employees can find specific information and answers to questions. (See Murphy & Swenson, "20 Questions to Ask About Your Code of Conduct," *ethikos* 17 no. 1 (July/Aug. 2003): 7-8.)

3 **Q&A.** Include Q&A in the code, to provide examples and answer common questions. (See Murphy & Swenson, "20 Questions to Ask About Your Code of Conduct," 17 *ethikos* no. 7 (July/Aug. 2003): 8; Singer, "UPS Translates and Transports an Ethics Code Overseas," *ethikos* 14 no.6, (May/June 2001): 1-2.)

4   **Reader-friendly formatting.** Use formatting elements that appear in popular media publications. These would include pullouts, bullets, graphics and illustrations. For a pullout you take key language from a page and put it in a highlight box so even casual readers will see it. Bullets are used to emphasize important elements in the code. Likewise, graphics and illustrations are used to make the code more interesting and draw attention to key points.

5   **Famous quotes.** Use quotes from inspirational leaders at various points in the code. (See Singer, "How the World Bank Revised its Code of Conduct," *ethikos* 15 no. 3, (Nov./Dec. 2001): 4, 6.)

6   **Reference information.** Include in the code contact details for sources of further information related to code provisions. For example, the code could include related policies and guides, Web sites, and e-mail and phone numbers of subject-matter experts. (See Singer, "Packaging an Ethics Code: Altria Learns That One Size Doesn't Fit All," *ethikos* 18 no. 4 (Jan/Feb 2005): 4, 7; Walker, "New Code Requirements: Preliminary Answers to Some Emerging Questions," *ethikos* 18 no. 2, (Sept./Oct. 2004): 1, 5.)

7   **CEO letter.** Have a letter from the CEO endorsing the code and compliance program, in his or her own language, and using a personal story as part of the endorsement.

8   **Code as a constitution.** Treat the code like a constitution, setting out the important elements common to most or all employees, to cover fundamental points. (See HHS, "OIG Compliance Program Guidance for Pharmaceutical Manufacturers," *Federal Register*, 68, no. 23 (May 5, 2003): 731, 733.)

9   **Test comprehension.** Test the reading comprehension level of the code. Will employees understand what they are supposed to do?

10 **Involvement in creating the code.** Have directors, managers, and employees at all levels be involved in the development of the code. (See HHS, "OIG Compliance Program Guidance for Pharmaceutical Manufacturers," *Federal Register* 68, (May 5, 2003): 23,731, 23,733.)

11 **SME input.** Have the risk area subject matter experts (SMEs) review the code to ensure their risk areas are appropriately covered. (See Singer, "How the World Bank Revised its Code of Conduct," *ethikos* 15 no. 3 (Nov./Dec. 2001): 4-5.)

12 **Online comment period.** Put the draft code online and invite all employees to provide input and comments. (See Singer, "How the World Bank Revised its Code of Conduct," *ethikos* 15 no. 3 (Nov./Dec. 2001): 4-5.)

13 **Regional advisory councils.** For multinational companies, have national or regional advisory councils provide input on the code so it is consistent with various cultures and national requirements. (See Singer, "UPS Translates and Transports an Ethics Code Overseas," *ethikos* 14 no. 6 (May/June 2001): 1.)

14 **Regional sections or supplements.** Add local sections or supplements to the code to meet different regional or national legal requirements and cultural elements. (See Singer, "UPS Translates and Transports an Ethics Code Overseas," *ethikos* 14 no. 6 (May/June 2001): 1-2.)

15 **Code for non-managers.** Do a separate code for non-management employees, e.g., retail store clerks, manufacturing plant workers. (See Singer, "Packaging an Ethics Code: Altria Learns That One Size Doesn't Fit All," *ethikos* 18 no. 4 (Jan/Feb 2005): 4.)

16 **Focus group reviews.** Have focus groups throughout the company review and comment on the code. (See Singer, "Packaging an Ethics Code: Altria Learns That One Size Doesn't Fit All," *ethikos* 18 no. 4 (Jan/Feb 2005): 4.)

17 **Code celebration.** Have the launch of the code be an event, with a celebration and gathering together of company employees. (See Singer, "How the World Bank Revised its Code of Conduct," *ethikos* 15 no. 3 (Nov./Dec. 2001): 4-5.)

18 **Mail to homes.** Consider mailing the code to employees' homes. (See Singer, "Bracing for Deregulation, AEP Boosts Ethics Training," *ethikos* 11 no. 1 (July/Aug. 1997): 1-2.)

19 **Code on the intranet.** Put the finished code on the company's intranet so that it can be searched and printed easily. (See Murphy & Swenson, "20 Questions to Ask About Your Code of Conduct," *ethikos* 17 no. 1 (July/Aug. 2003): 7, 9.)

20 **Stakeholders.** Organize the code based on duties to various stakeholder groups, e.g., employees, customers, investors, etc.

21 **Supervisors' responsibilities.** Include coverage in the code of the special responsibilities of managers, such as the need to supervise subordinates' compliance with law and the code. (See Kaplan, "The Tone at the Middle," *ethikos* 20 no. 2 (Sept./Oct. 2006): 5-6.)

22 **Light colored paper.** Use light colored paper with dark print for the code. Dark paper, such as red paper, is difficult to copy, and you certainly want your employees copying things from the code. (See Murphy & Swenson, "20 Questions to Ask About Your Code of Conduct," *ethikos* 17 no. 1 (July/Aug. 2003): 7-8.)

23 **Translations.** When having an outside firm translate the code, have experts in the company who are native speakers check the translation. Also use "translation back," where a translated version is translated back to the original language to test the validity of the translation. (See Singer, "Packaging an Ethics Code: Altria Learns That One Size Doesn't Fit All," *ethikos* 18 no. 4 (Jan/Feb 2005): 4, 7; Singer, "UPS Translates and Transports an Ethics Code Overseas," *ethikos* 14 no. 6 (May/June 2001): 1, 3.)

24 **Blind employees.** Have a version of the code for the vision impaired, perhaps an audio code. (See Murphy & Swenson, "20 Questions to Ask About Your Code of Conduct," *ethikos* 17 no. 1 (July/Aug. 2003): 7, 9.)

25 **6 Sigma.** Use a 6 Sigma/project management approach to developing and rolling out the code. (See Singer, "Caterpillar's Code Revisions: Reinforcing the 'High' Way," *ethikos* 20 no. 2 (Sept./Oct. 2006): 8-9.)

26 **Disclaimers.** Use disclaimers for such legal issues as noting that the code does not create an employment contract with employees. (See Murphy & Swenson, "20 Questions to Ask About Your Code of Conduct," *ethikos* 17 no. 1 (July/Aug. 2003): 7-8.)

27 **Inventory of manuals.** When rolling out a new code, especially in newly-acquired companies and in foreign offices, do an inventory of existing policies, manuals, HR manuals, etc., to avoid conflicts with the new code. (See Murphy, "When Starting Your Compliance Program, Survey What's Already in Place—and in Practice," *ethikos* 16 no. 5 (Mar./Apr. 2003): 5.)

28 **Union input.** Consider reviewing a draft of the code with union officials (and works councils in Europe) for their input. This can increase buy in and may be legally required in some circumstances. (See Di Santo & Hengesbaugh, "U.S. Helplines Raise EU Privacy Concerns," *ethikos* 19 no. 2 (Sept./Oct. 2005): 1, 20.)

29 **Key questions.** Begin the code with "the questions" for employees to ask about their proposed conduct: Is it legal? Is it ethical (or right)? How would it look on the front page of the Wall Street Journal? (This is called the "newspaper test.") (See Murphy & Swenson, "20 Questions to Ask About Your Code of Conduct," *ethikos* 17 no. 1 (July/Aug. 2003): 7-8.)

30 **Managers' and employees' duties.** One approach for a code is to have one page explain what to expect of company management, and the facing page explain what the company expects of employees. (See Singer, "Packaging an Ethics Code: Altria Learns That One Size Doesn't Fit All," *ethikos* 18 no. 4 (Jan/Feb 2005): 4, 6.)

31 **Code to outside professionals.** Provide a copy of the code of conduct to professional services firms providing advice to the company, e.g., lawyers, accountants, etc., instructing them that the code represents the highest expression of the company's wishes, and that no services are to be provided to any company officer, director or employee that conflict with the provisions of the code.

32 **Certification.** Have employees certify that they have received, read, understood, and will comply with the code. (See Jordan & Murphy, "Compliance Programs: What the Government Really Wants," *ACCA Docket* (July/Aug. 1996): 10, 20; Sigler & Murphy, *Interactive Corporate Compliance: An Alternative to Regulatory Compulsion* (Westport, CT: Quorum Books, 1988): 84.)

33 **Online code training.** Have employees take code training online, and after completing the training certify online that they have read, understood and will abide by the code. (See Singer, "Coors Brewing Company's Ethics Code Training," ethikos 16 no. 2 (Sept./Oct. 2002): 4-5.)

34 **Code month.** Set one month per year as "code of conduct month," to celebrate and focus on the code. (See Murphy & McCollum, "Communicating 'in a Practical Manner:' Bell Atlantic's Report on Integrity," *Corporate Conduct Quarterly* (now *ethikos*) 4 (1996): 59.)

35 **Waivers.** Have a system developed in advance for handling code waiver requests, especially those involving officers and board members. (See Walker, "New Code Requirements: Preliminary Answers to Some Emerging Questions," *ethikos* 18 no. 2 (Sept./Oct. 2004): 1-2.)

36 **Business unit guides.** Have each business unit develop its own guide for employee conduct, in addition to the corporate code of conduct, to address issues particular to that business unit. (See Singer, "Sara Lee Corporation Relies on its Business Practices Officers Overseas," *ethikos* 11 no. 3 (Nov./Dec. 1997): 4, 12.)

37 **Compliance program policy.** Have a corporate policy for implementing the details of the compliance program. This would be the next level of documentation after a board resolution.

38 **Inventory policies.** Conduct an inventory and review of all corporate policies touching on areas related to compliance, to ensure consistency and to add appropriate cross references to the code and the compliance and ethics program.

39 **HR manual.** If there is a separate HR manual or personnel policy, review these documents and ensure consistency with the code and the compliance and ethics program.

40 **Policy overload.** Compile all the company compliance policies, eliminate the unnecessary ones and prune others so they are more manageable, readable, and useful for employees. (See Nortz, "Unread, Codes of Conduct Become Dangerous Dust Collectors," *ethikos* 19 no. 4 (Jan./Feb. 2006): 9, 11.)

41 **Policy implementation.** Require that every corporate policy relating to compliance include a section stating who will be responsible for implementing the policy, and how they will communicate it to employees. Have this implementation included in the audit process, so it is reviewed periodically.

B. USSGs Item 1, compliance controls

USSGs item 1 not only covers policies, but also procedures. As explained in the Sentencing Guidelines commentary, procedures include the use of controls. The ideas here cover the area of compliance-related controls.

42 **Rotation.** Use a rotation policy in key control positions to reduce the risks of corruption or a compromise of security. (See Murphy, "Reducing Foreign Corrupt Practices Act Risk: An Effective Self-Policing Program," *Corporate Conduct Quarterly* (now *ethikos*) 5 (1996): 28, 30.)

43 **Division of functions.** Divide job responsibilities, so no one person has too much unchecked authority over money and important decisions. (See Murphy, "Lost Words of the Sentencing Guidelines," *ethikos* 16 no. 3 (Nov./Dec. 2002): 5-6.)

44 **Require centralized approvals.** For certain high-risk activities, require headquarters' advance approval. Consultation with a specific compliance risk expert may also be required.

45 **Mandatory legal department review/approval.** For certain high-risk activities, require prior legal department review and approval, or at least consultation. (See Sigler & Murphy, *Interactive Corporate Compliance: An Alternative to Regulatory Compulsion* (Westport, CT: Quorum Books, 1988): 88, 90.)

46 **Limits on outside systems.** In order to facilitate compliance monitoring, require that all business-related communications and records be conducted only through company systems that are open to review and audit.

47 **Prevention consultants.** Have compliance and ethics professionals review new business proposals and operations to analyze where problems could occur and where control weaknesses might exist, and recommend controls tailored to the potential risks. (See Roach & Davis, "Establishing a Culture of Ethics and Integrity in Government," *ethikos* 21 no. 2 (Sept./Oct. 2007): 1, 16.)

48 **Level of authorization.** For certain high risk areas, require that the level of authority for approval be equivalent to the dollar risk associated with a potential violation. (See Sigler & Murphy, *Interactive Corporate Compliance: An Alternative to Regulatory Compulsion* (Westport, CT: Quorum Books, 1988): 90; Lipson, "A Survey on the Ins and Outs of Antitrust Compliance," *Antitrust Law Journal* 51 (1982): 517.)

49 **Multiple signatures.** For expenditures above certain levels, and for authorizations involving higher risks, require two or more signatures that include managers not in the same line of command.

50 **Mandatory vacation.** Require those in positions involving important controls, handling of cash or other transactions, and other sensitive positions to take periodic vacations of at least a week away from the office. This can make it impossible to cover-up misconduct. (See Goldfarb, Cass & Sanati, "Too Many Days on the Job," *Wall Street Journal* (Jan. 29, 2008): C14; Murphy, "Reducing Foreign Corrupt Practices Act Risk: An Effective Self-Policing Program," *Corporate Conduct Quarterly* (now *ethikos*) 5 (1996): 28, 30.)

C. USSGs item 2, compliance officer and infrastructure

For the compliance and ethics program to work, there must be a compliance and ethics officer, and the necessary compliance infrastructure to make the program successful. These points address part of the area covered under item 2 of the USSGs.

51 **Employment contract.** Have an employment contract for the compliance officer. (See Murphy, "Enhancing the Compliance Officer's Authority: Preparing an Employment Contract," *ethikos* 11 no.5 (May/June 1998): 5.)

52 **CCEP certification.** Have the compliance officer and staff get "Certified in Compliance and Ethics Professional" (CCEP) certification. (See the Society of Corporate Compliance and Ethics Web site, www.corporatecompliance.org; Leet, "A New Compliance Certification Program," *ethikos* 20 no.4 (Jan/Feb 2007): 15.)

53 **Compliance program lawyer.** Have a senior-level lawyer designated as the lawyer for the compliance program, to develop expertise in the compliance and ethics area and provide support to the compliance officer. (See Murphy, "Chapter 10: Protections for Compliance People," in Murphy & Leet, *Working for Integrity* (Minneapolis: Society of Corporate Compliance and Ethics, 2006): 397-416.)

54 **Workshops for C&E professionals.** Provide seminars and workshops for compliance and ethics people throughout the company, including those in the business units and those involved in the risk areas. These can cover the "how to" of compliance and ethics work, and the various compliance risk areas. (See Singer, "Needed from Bertelsmann's Ethics & Compliance Officer: A 'Diplomatic Effort,'" *ethikos* 17 no. 2 (Sept./Oct. 2003): 7, 9.)

55 **C&E training for HR.** Provide specially focused training about the compliance and ethics program for HR people, explaining what the program is, how it relates to HR, and the importance of HR's role in making the program effective. This is important because so many HR functions affect the compliance and ethics program.

56 **Responsible executives.** Have a senior manager responsible for each compliance risk area; this person would be the executive responsible for ensuring that the compliance work in that risk area was effective. The executive would not necessarily be the risk area subject-matter expert. (See Kaplan, "Sundstrand's 'Responsible Executive' Program," *Corporate Conduct Quarterly* (now *ethikos*) 4 (1996): 33.)

57 **SMEs.** Have experts in each risk area assigned as the subject matter experts (SMEs) for those areas, e.g., antitrust, privacy, money-laundering, etc. The SMEs would work with the compliance officer and ensure that their areas are appropriately covered by compliance efforts. (See Singer, "Exelon Excels at Reaching Out," *ethikos* 16 no. 6 (May/June 2003): 7.)

58 **SME councils.** Have a committee or council made up of those responsible for the compliance efforts in all of the different compliance risk areas. This committee could meet periodically to assess and coordinate compliance efforts in the different risk areas. (See Scarpino, "NCR Corporation's Four-fold Ethics & Compliance Model," *ethikos* 20 no. 1 (July/Aug. 2006): 7, 9, 17.)

59 **SME plans.** Require an annual plan for compliance efforts in each compliance risk area, e.g., export control, EEO, antitrust, etc. If there are responsible executives or other subject matter experts, they would be responsible for preparing the plans.

60 **SME compliance committees.** Have a committee of managers and experts addressing certain high risk areas, such as health and safety, and environmental compliance. For example, there might be a safety committee, an environmental compliance committee and/or a privacy committee. (See Kaplan, "The Boss's New Job: Ensuring Compliance Program Effectiveness," *ethikos* 18 no. 6 (May/June, 2005): 1, 12.)

61 **Escalation guidelines.** Establish and publicize guidelines throughout the company, describing the types of allegations that must be centrally reported to the chief compliance officer, so that this officer can ensure appropriate matters are reported to the board.

62 **Assistant compliance officer.** Have a second in command for the program, to handle administrative matters and act in the compliance officer's absence. This is especially important if the compliance officer has other responsibilities besides compliance and ethics. (See Petry, "EOA Survey: Companies Seeking to Integrate Ethics Through the Whole Organization," *ethikos* 15 no. 1 (July/Aug. 2001): 1-2.)

63 **Interdepartmental compliance committee**. Have an interdepartmental compliance committee, including members from key departments (e.g., HR, legal, internal audit, IT, etc.) and from the business units, with sufficient authority to make commitments for their departments/units. (See Scarpino, "NCR Corporation's Four-fold Ethics & Compliance Model," *ethikos* 20 no. 1 (July/Aug. 2006): 7-8; Jordan & Murphy, "Compliance Programs: What the Government Really Wants," *ACCA Docket* (July/Aug. 1996):10, 15-16; Kaplan, "The Boss's New Job: Ensuring Compliance Program Effectiveness," *ethikos* 18 no. 6 (May/June, 2005): 1, 3; HHS, "OIG Compliance Program Guidance for Pharmaceutical Manufacturers," *Federal Register* 68,(May 5, 2003): 23,731, 23,740, 23,743.)

64 **Committee meeting schedules.** Have the interdepartmental compliance committee schedule its meetings prior to the audit committee's meetings. The compliance committee then feeds into the compliance officer's report to the audit committee. This helps avoid postponing the compliance committee's meetings, and can enhance attendance.

65 **Compliance committee training.** Provide training to the compliance committee members about the compliance and ethics program, and their responsibilities as committee members. This could be done by setting aside a specific amount of time for training at each meeting. (See HHS, "OIG Compliance Program Guidance for Pharmaceutical Manufacturers," *Federal Register* 68 (May 5, 2003): 23,731, 23,740.; Charles E. Colitre.)

66 **Field participation.** Invite field managers to participate in compliance committee meetings to bring fresh perspectives, and to spread understanding about the compliance and ethics program.

67 **Open ethics committee.** Have an ethics committee composed of senior managers who meet to discuss ethics issues facing the company, and allow employees to attend the meetings and see the process. (See Singer, "The 1950s: Eisenhower, the Yankees, Senator McCarthy and an Ethics Committee," *ethikos* 15 no. 2 (Sept./Oct. 2001): 11.)

68 **Ethics council.** Consider an ethics advisory council that includes union leaders and non-management employees who meet to discuss and advise on ethics issues. (See Singer, "Born of strife, DTE's heterogeneous ethics council advises," *ethikos* 15 no. 6 (May/June 2002): 9.)

69 **Business unit C&E officials.** Have compliance officials designated in all subsidiaries and business units. (See Murphy, "Facility Compliance Coordinator Position Could Help Ensure That Compliance Program Reaches the Field," *Prevention of Corporate Liability Current Report* 4 (Dec. 16, 1996): 12; Scarpino, "NCR Corporation's Four-Fold Ethics & Compliance Model," *ethikos* 20 no. 1 (July/Aug. 2006): 7, 9.)

70 **Facility compliance and ethics officials.** Require a compliance and ethics person be assigned for each substantial company physical facility. This model is prevalent in safety programs. (See Jordan & Murphy, "Compliance Programs: What the Government Really Wants," *ACCA Docket* (July/Aug. 1996): 10, 15; *In re Grumman Corp.*, settlement agreement (E.D.N.Y., Nov. 23, 1993).)

71 **Business unit compliance committees.** Have compliance or business practices committees in the business units composed of senior officials and the business unit compliance manager. Have the minutes of each business unit compliance committee meeting sent to the chief compliance officer and/or the corporate compliance committee. (See Singer, "Sara Lee Corporation Relies on its Business Practices Officers Overseas," *ethikos* 11 no. 3 (Nov./Dec. 1997): 4, 12; Singer, "Motorola's Ethics Renewal Process," *ethikos* 12 no. 1 (July/Aug. 1998): 4-5.)

72 **CO authority over remote compliance officials.** Give the compliance and ethics officer at least some level of authority over the business unit compliance officials, such as control over their removal, and input into their evaluations.

73 **Global compliance and ethics councils.** Have a council or committee of business unit compliance officials that meets periodically and exchanges best practices and other information. (See Scarpino, "NCR Corporation's Four-fold Ethics & Compliance Model," *ethikos* 20 no. 1 (July/Aug. 2006): 7.)

74 **Outside professional services.** Give the compliance officer full authority to retain professional services, including legal counsel, to assist in carrying out the program. This could be set out in the board resolution establishing the program.

75 **Global compliance conference.** For global companies, have a worldwide meeting or forum of the company's compliance and ethics people, to share experiences and best practices from the company's different business units. (See Singer, "The Timken Company Assesses its Worldwide Compliance Conference," *ethikos* 11 no. 5 (Mar./Apr. 1998): 5.)

76 **Summer interns.** Hire a summer intern from a college or graduate program to assist in the compliance program. This may also aid in recruiting future talent. (See Daly, "Ethics Programs and the Changes in the Boardroom," *ethikos* 14 no. 2 (Sept./Oct. 2000): 4, 6.)

77 **Mission statement.** Have a separate mission statement for the compliance program and the compliance and ethics organization.

78 **SMEs reporting to board.** Have each of the different compliance risk area subject matter experts and/or responsible executives report occasionally to the board/board committee on their portion of the compliance and ethics program.

79 **Business unit reports to the board.** Have each of the various business unit compliance and ethics program leaders report occasionally to the board/board committee on the status of the compliance and ethics program in their units.

80 **Sales skills.** Train all compliance and ethics managers on effective communications and sales skills, to help them in promoting the program. (See "Chapter 10: Selling Compliance (and the Importance of Your Job) to Management," in Murphy & Leet, *Building a Career in Compliance and Ethics* (Minneapolis: Society of Corporate Compliance and Ethics, 2007): 145-57.)

81 **IT expert.** Have an IT expert as part of the compliance and ethics team to help cover risks raised by new technology, and to assist in using technology for compliance and ethics purposes. Having a compliance champion in the IT department helps in many important ways.

82 **Helpers' position descriptions.** Include support of the compliance and ethics program in the position descriptions for those in other departments who play a role in the compliance and ethics program, e.g., lawyers, HR, IT, auditors, etc. This support would also be part of their objectives and evaluations.

83 **Business unit program manual.** Have a compliance program manual for guidance for the compliance and ethics people in all business units and risk areas. It can explain how to do each of the compliance functions, e.g., training, distributing the code, self-assessments, etc., and provide other resources such as contact names and numbers. (See Sigler & Murphy, *Interactive Corporate Compliance: An Alternative to Regulatory Compulsion* (Westport, CT: Quorum Books, 1988): 85.)

84 **Business unit status reports.** Require each business unit compliance officer/leader to report periodically and in writing to the chief compliance and ethics officer on the status of the unit's program.

85 **C&E professional ethics.** Have the company formally agree to abide by the professional ethical standards applicable to its compliance and ethics staff, i.e., the SCCE Code of Ethics. This goal could be reached by such means as inclusion in employment contracts, a board of directors' resolution, or inclusion in position descriptions. (See *SCCE Code of Ethics*, (Minneapolis: Society of Corporate Compliance and Ethics, 2007), http://www.corporatecompliance.org/Content/NavigationMenu/Resources/ProfessionalCode/SCCECodeofEthics.pdf; Murphy, "Chapter 10: Protections for Compliance People," in Murphy & Leet, *Working for Integrity: Finding the Perfect Job in the Rapidly-Growing Compliance and Ethics Field* (Minneapolis: Society of Corporate Compliance and Ethics, 2006): 397-416.)

86 **C&E career path.** Provide a structured career path for compliance and ethics professionals in your company. (See Murphy & Leet, "Chapter 14: Advice for Companies: Finding the Right Person for Your Compliance Positions," in *Working for Integrity: Finding the Perfect Job in the Rapidly-Growing Compliance and Ethics Field* (Minneapolis: Society of Corporate Compliance and Ethics, 2006): 485-510.)

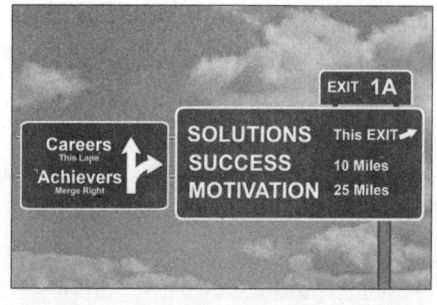

87 **Titles.** Get ideas for the job titles for your organization's chief compliance officer and other compliance and ethics positions by seeing what titles other organizations use—a list of more than 800 appears in Murphy & Leet, *Working for Integrity* (Minneapolis: Society of Corporate Compliance and Ethics, 2006): 65-90.)

88 **Position descriptions.** Have position descriptions for compliance and ethics professionals that require substantial experience and competence in the relevant compliance and ethics areas. (See Jordan & Murphy, "Compliance Programs: What the Government Really Wants," *ACCA Docket* (July/Aug. 1996):10, 15.)

89 **Empowerment.** One element of the compliance professional's empowerment is having sufficient security to act from a position of strength. Provide compliance professionals with indemnification, insurance, and a severance package. (See Murphy, "Chapter 10: Protections for Compliance People," in Murphy & Leet, *Working for Integrity* (Minneapolis: Society of Corporate Compliance and Ethics, 2006): 397-416; Murphy, "Questions to Ask About an In-House Compliance and Ethics Job offer," *ethikos* 18 no. 3 (Nov./Dec. 2004): 7, 9.)

90 **Direct access.** Provide in clear corporate policies that the compliance officer has direct access to the CEO, board of directors, all senior managers, and legal counsel. (See HHS, "OIG Compliance Program Guidance for Pharmaceutical Manufacturers," *Federal Register* 68 no. 23 (May 5, 2003): 731, 739.)

91 **Access to records.** Provide that the compliance officer has direct, unrestricted access to all documents and other records. (See HHS, "OIG Compliance Program Guidance for Pharmaceutical Manufacturers," *Federal Register* 68 (May 5, 2003): 23,731, 23,739.)

92 **Checks and balances.** Maintain a system of checks and balances by separating control functions. The compliance officer would report neither to the general counsel nor to the officer responsible for financial controls. (See HHS, "OIG Compliance Program Guidance for Pharmaceutical Manufacturers," *Federal Register* 68 (May 5, 2003): 23,731, 23,743.)

D. USSGs item 2, the board and senior management

Compliance professionals cannot make a compliance and ethics program work; this goal takes the support of the board and management. These ideas cover this important part of any program, and cover points under item 2 of the USSGs.

93 **Board resolution.** Have the board adopt a resolution establishing and empowering the compliance and ethics program. Publish the board's compliance resolution in the company's annual report/proxy statement. (See Singer, "AEP's Ethics Interviews Are 'About the Passion of the People,'" *ethikos* 13 no. 6 (May/June 2000): 1, 3; Murphy, "Chapter 10: Protections for Compliance People," in Murphy & Leet, *Working for Integrity* (Minneapolis: Society of Corporate Compliance and Ethics, 2006): 397-416.)

94 **CO appointed by board.** Have the compliance officer appointed by the board, as part of a board resolution. (See Murphy, "Compliance Officers: One Part Ombudsman, Two Parts Watchdog," *National Law Journal* (Dec. 14, 1992): S2.)

95 **CO Exit interview.** Have the board or audit committee conduct an exit interview of a departing compliance and ethics officer. This tactic could also be extended to direct reports of that officer. (From Dan Roach and Jeff Kaplan.)

96 **Board code of conduct.** Have board members officially adopt the code of conduct as applying to them, and certify that they are in compliance. (See Jordan & Murphy, "Compliance Programs: What the Government Really Wants," *ACCA Docket* (July/Aug. 1996): 10, 14.)

97 **CO in key meetings.** The board can specify that the compliance officer shall participate in all executive meetings, including strategic, operational and review meetings of the CEO's executive management team, and has input into significant business decisions. (See Petry, "Assessing Corporate Culture: Part II," *ethikos* 19 no. 1 (July/Aug. 2005): 10, 13.)

98 **Board committee.** Have a committee of independent directors responsible for monitoring the compliance and ethics program. This is often the audit committee, although some companies have a separate committee with only this responsibility. (See "Chronikos," *ethikos* 19 no. 5 (Mar./Apr. 2006): 10.)

99 **Board question list.** Provide board members with a list of questions for assessing the company's compliance and ethics program. (See office of Inspector General of the U.S. Department of Health and Human Services and the American Health Lawyers Association, *Corporate Responsibility and Corporate Compliance: A Resource for Health Care Boards of Directors* (Office of Inspector General of the U.S. Department of Health and Human Services, 2003), http://oig.hhs.gov/fraud/docs/complianceguidance/040203CorpRespRsceGuide.pdf; Kaplan, "Post-Enron Expectations: Directors, Investigations and Independence of Process," *ethikos* 17 no.1 (July/Aug. 2003): 1.)

100 **Compliance officer on board.** Have the board recruit a compliance officer from another company to be a board member. (See Murphy & Roach, "Compliance Officer on Board: What Your Audit Committee is Missing," *ethikos* 20 no. 3 (Nov/Dec 2006): 12.)

101 **Background for the board.** Have an outside compliance and ethics expert provide the board with background about compliance and ethics programs, including the board's role in supervising the program.

102 **Subsidiary boards.** Require boards of major subsidiaries to have ethics/compliance committees to address compliance and ethics issues in that business unit. (See Singer, "Values is the Bedrock Upon Which Suez Builds," *ethikos* 15 no. 3 (Nov./Dec. 2001): 11.)

103 **CEO executive meetings.** The CEO can show support for the program by going around the table at his or her executive meetings and having each senior officer report on what he or she has done specifically to promote the compliance and ethics program in his/her business unit. The compliance and ethics officer would be there as a reality check. (See Murphy, "How the CEO Can Make the Difference in Compliance and Ethics," *ethikos* 20 no. 6 (May/June 2007): 9.)

104 **CEO networking.** The CEO can network with his/her peers at other companies on ways to promote compliance and ethics. (See Murphy, "How the CEO Can Make the Difference in Compliance and Ethics," *ethikos* 20 no. 6 (May/June 2007): 9.)

105 **CEO ethics visits.** Have the CEO travel to each business unit for a face-to-face meeting with the business unit head, the unit's legal counsel, and the local compliance and ethics person, to discuss compliance and ethics. (See Singer, "Shell Oil Company 'Energizes' its Ethics Commitment," *ethikos* 16 no. 3 (Nov./Dec. 2002): 8, 9.)

106 **Take your CO to lunch.** Something as simple as taking the compliance officer to lunch can help empower the compliance officer. A board member could do this to enhance communications; the CEO could do this, especially in the company cafeteria, to send a message of support for the program.

107　**Board engagement.** To get a feel for the company's compliance and ethics culture, board members can talk with employees and get a first hand sense of how they see the company's values. (See Singer, "Solomon Ex-CEO Denham: Board Has Key Oversight Role in Ethics & Compliance," *ethikos* 21 no. 2 (Sept./Oct. 2007): 13.)

108　**Directors speak out.** Have members of the board of directors help communicate the compliance and ethics message by speaking or being interviewed in a company compliance and ethics newsletter. (See Kaplan, "The Board's Role in Ethics Programs: a Global Study," *ethikos* 17 no. 5 (Mar./Apr. 2004): 1, 4.)

109　**Dog-eared code.** Have the CEO keep a used, dog-eared copy of the company's code of conduct on the top of his/her desk and make a point of using and referring to it. (See Murphy, "How the CEO Can Make the Difference in Compliance and Ethics," *ethikos* 20 no. 6 (May/June 2007): 9.)

110　**CEO as program model.** The CEO can make a point of being the model in the compliance program. Examples include taking the employee training first, doing a safety walk-through, calling the company helpline with a question, calling and asking a field line manager about his/her role in the code of conduct roll-out and training, and attending an SCCE program as a participant (not a speaker). (See Murphy, "How the CEO Can Make the Difference in Compliance and Ethics," 20 *ethikos* no. 6 (May/June 2007): 9.)

111　**CEO in regular training sessions.** Have the CEO attend one of the regular compliance training sessions with rank-and-file employees. (See "Walking the Talk," *ethikos* 16 no. 5 (Mar./April 2003): 12.)

112　**Start training at the top.** The compliance training could start by training first the senior executives who report directly to the CEO. (See Singer, "Ethics Training at Lockheed Martin Takes a Tabloid Turn," *ethikos* 15 no. 1 (July/Aug. 2001): 8-9.)

113 **Training for the board.** Arrange compliance and ethics training for the board, covering both the compliance and ethics program, and the board's substantive risk areas. Publicize the facts about this training, so employees know the board also takes the training. (See Hoffman, Driscoll & Rowe, "Effective Ethics Education of the Board," *ethikos* 18 no. 1 (Jan./Feb. 2005): 16; Kaplan, "The Board's Role in Ethics Programs: a Global Study," *ethikos* 17 no. 5 (Mar./Apr. 2004): 1, 4.)

114 **New director orientation.** Provide an orientation session for new board members, explaining the company's compliance and ethics program, covering the company's compliance and ethics risks, and explaining the board member's duties in this context. (See Walker, "The NYSE Report: Analyzing its Impact on Corporate Compliance Programs," *ethikos* 16 no. 1 (July/Aug. 2002): 1, 13.)

115 **Mandatory board reports.** Have mandatory reporting by the compliance officer to the board on key points, including any allegations about senior officers or rejection of the compliance officer's advice. (See Singer, "An Ethics Officer of Olympian Proportions," *ethikos* 18 no. 2 (Sept./Oct. 2004): 6, 8.)

116 **Board control.** Have all decisions affecting the compliance officer's employment by the company, including hiring, transfer, termination and similar matters, and any decision limiting the scope of the program, require the prior approval of the board. (See Murphy, "Chapter 10: Protections for Compliance People," in Murphy & Leet, *Working for Integrity* (Minneapolis: Society of Corporate Compliance and Ethics, 2006): 397-416.)

117 **C&E expert for the board.** Provide the audit committee of the board with access to a compliance and ethics expert independent from management and the company's own compliance program. This helps in assessing the effectiveness of the compliance and ethics program.

118 **CO audit committee access.** Provide the compliance officer with unrestricted access to the audit committee in executive session. This tactic could also include setting a minimum number of pre-scheduled executive meetings with the compliance officer. (See Kaplan, "The Boss's New Job: Ensuring Compliance Program Effectiveness," *ethikos* 18 no. 6 (May/June, 2005): 1, 3.; Dan Roach.)

119 **Tone at the middle.** In addition to having senior management publicly support the compliance and ethics program, include a focus on compliance and ethics for middle management, who set the tone for most workers. (See Singer, "KPMG Seeks to Propel Ethics to the 'Ends of the Tentacles,'" *ethikos* 21 no. 3 (Nov./Dec. 2007): 4-5; Kaplan, "The Tone at the Middle," *ethikos* 20 no. 2 (Sept./Oct. 2006): 5.)

120 **Agent for the board.** Have the compliance officer designated as the "agent for the board," acting directly on behalf of the board to promote compliance and ethical conduct. Care must be taken, however, to ensure that this officer is not perceived as a spy. (See Hoffman & Rowe, "The Ethics Officer and the Board: Partners for Effective Ethical Governance," *ethikos* 21 no. 2 (Sept./Oct. 2007): 8.)

121 **Reporting to the board.** Have the chief compliance and ethics officer not only formally "report" to the board, but also have more informal and ongoing relationships with individual board members, including the chair of the audit committee. (See Sherwood, "The Evolving Position of Ethics Officer," *ethikos* 20 no. 1, (July/Aug. 2006): 10, 18.)

122 **"Invitations" to visit the board.** If a business unit is lagging in its compliance and ethics efforts, have the board's audit or compliance committee "invite" the unit's senior manager to discuss the unit's compliance and ethics program's progress. (See Singer, "Marsh's Business Reforms: Much Ground Covered in Little Time," *ethikos* 19 no. 6 (May/June 2006): 1, 3-4.)

123 **Responsibility for compliance.** Specify in the code, corporate policy or other important and widely-read document, that responsibility for actual compliance and ethical conduct is squarely on the shoulders of each employee, and especially managers, and not the compliance and ethics officer. (See *U.S. Sentencing Guidelines*, Section 8B2.1 (b)(2)(B).)

E. Winning management over

For a compliance and ethics program to work, it needs support all up and down the line, from the top of the corporate structure to the employees on the front line. Here are ideas and information to use for convincing the board, management and the employees to support the program.

124 **Fines.** Fines for violations have become astronomical. Just as one example, U.S. antitrust fines were recently increased from $10 million to $100 million. Fines in the hundreds of millions are now imposed for corporate crimes.

125 **Other penalties.** Even where the penalties imposed are not technically "criminal," the financial impact can be enormous. For example, the E.U. has been imposing civil penalties in 9 figures for violations of E.U. competition law; enforcers have authority to impose penalties equal to 10% of annual turnover.

126 **Prison.** Like fines, prison terms for white collar crimes have also been escalating, and in the U.S. federal system there is no parole.

127 **Suspension and debarment.** Government contractors who commit compliance violations can lose their ability to do business with the government.

128 **"Voluntary disclosure."** It can be enlightening to managers and employees to discover how the government finds out about corporate crimes. Point out that the voluntary disclosure programs, where one's partner in crime gets off by turning you in, is a frequent way that corporate crime gets uncovered.

129 **Qui tam.** Whistle-blower provisions for government contractors offer enormous rewards to those individuals, including employees, who turn in evidence of false claims activities.

130 **Reducing fines.** One reason for having a program is the reduction in fines provided under the USSGs for companies with effective programs, should the company get in trouble. This achievement, along with steps like cooperating with the government, can reduce fines by as much as 95%.

131 **Reducing waste, fraud and abuse.** The same program steps designed to prevent harm by the company help to prevent harm *to* the company. Waste, fraud and abuse can cost a company dearly; helplines, controls, audits, monitoring, etc., help reduce this cost.

132 **Avoiding prosecution.** An effective program can persuade prosecutors not to indict or otherwise prosecute a company. (See Baylson, "Getting the Demons Into Heaven: A Good Corporate Compliance Program," *Corporate Conduct Quarterly* (now *ethikos*) 2 (Winter 1992): 33.)

133 **Defense to liability.** In certain areas of the law, a compliance program may be a defense to liability.

134 **Defense to punitive damages.** Compliance programs may also serve as a basis for avoiding punitive damages.

135 **Avoiding probation and DPAs.** Companies can have compliance programs and government-arranged supervision imposed on them for violations. An effective program already in existence can help avoid this penalty, or at least ameliorate what is required.

136 **Protect the brand.** A corporate scandal can severely damage or destroy the value of a brand built up over years of hard work.

137 **Protect the board.** Under the *Caremark* case, board members could potentially face liability if there is a violation that harms the company and a program could have prevented the loss. (See *In re Caremark International Inc. Derivative Litigation*, 698 A.2d 959 (Del. Ch. 1996).)

138 **It's not optional.** More and more, compliance programs are being mandated by governments and stock exchanges. It makes sense to get ahead of this trend. (See Murphy, "'Mandavolent' Compliance," *ethikos* 19 no. 2 (Sept./Oct. 2005): 8.)

139 **We're already partly there.** Companies do not have to start from scratch. Often there are compliance program elements already in place, but not recognized as such. Why not get credit for what you are already doing? (See Murphy, "When Starting Your Compliance Program, Survey What's Already in Place—and in Practice," *ethikos* 16 no. 5 (Mar./Apr. 2003): 5.)

140 **A marketing advantage.** For blue chip companies, the fact that a potential supplier has a strong compliance program may be a source of comfort and a marketing advantage. It helps show the potential supplier is trustworthy. (See Kaplan, "Compliance Programs For Smaller Companies," *ethikos* 21 no. 4 (Jan./Feb. 2008): 6; Parmenter, "Eight Reasons Smaller Companies Should Have Compliance Programs," *ethikos* 18 no. 2 (Sept./Oct. 2004): 9-10.)

141 **Recruit top people.** After Enron, employees have had increased concern about the integrity of the company they work for. Potential board members also want to know they are joining a reputable company. A vigorous program can help in recruiting and retaining employees. (See Parmenter, "Eight Reasons Smaller Companies Should Have Compliance Programs," *ethikos* 18 no. 2 (Sept./Oct. 2004): 9-10; Berg, "Ethics and the Inclusion of the Virtual Workforce," *ethikos* 14 no. 2 (Sept./Oct. 2000): 7-8.)

142 **It's a global trend.** This is an international trend, with companies all over the world implementing programs, and governments and stock exchanges in a number of countries encouraging and/or requiring this. (See the international section of the SCCE Web site, http://www.corporatecompliance.org/AM/Template.cfm?Section=International; Bevilacqua, "Corporate Compliance Programs Under Italian Law," 20 *ethikos* no. 1 (Nov./Dec.2006); "Chapter 21: Globalizing the Compliance Program: Why and How," in Kaplan & Murphy, *Compliance Programs and the Corporate Sentencing Guidelines* (Eagan, MN: Thomson/West. 1993 & Ann'l Supp).)

143 **It's the right thing to do.** Not everyone in business is cynical. One strong argument for having a program is that it is the right thing to do as a responsible corporate citizen.

144 **Going public.** For privately owned companies looking to go public, having a compliance program may be a prerequisite to being listed and a factor for determining the risk level of the business for underwriting purposes. (See Parmenter, "Eight Reasons Smaller Companies Should Have Compliance Programs," *ethikos* 18 no. 2 (Sept./Oct. 2004): 9-10.)

145 **More ideas.** For more ideas and further details on how to emphasize the benefits of compliance and ethics programs, see Murphy & Leet, *Building a Career in Compliance and Ethics*, "Chapter 10: Selling Compliance (and the Importance of Your Job) to Management" (Minneapolis: Society of Corporate Compliance and Ethics, 2007): 145-157.)

F. USSGs item 3, background checks, diligence in hiring, and promotions

A compliance and ethics program needs to avoid giving authority to those likely to break the law. The points here address the elements of USSGs item 3.

146 **Review of promotions.** Clear significant promotions with the compliance office. The compliance office would know if a potential promotion involved someone who was under investigation for misconduct that should disqualify the person from promotion. (See "Monitoring and Input on Promotions," in *Building Incentives in Your Compliance & Ethics Program* (Minneapolis: Society of Corporate Compliance and Ethics, 2007), http://www.corporatecompliance.org/Content/NavigationMenu/Resources/IssuesAnswers/DRAFTwhitepaper-BuildingIncentivesCompliance_WOappdx.pdf; Sigler & Murphy, *Interactive Corporate Compliance: An Alternative to Regulatory Compulsion* (Westport, CT: Quorum Books, 1988): 90.)

147 **Check résumés.** Check the items in an applicant's résumé as a check on honesty. (See Sherwood, "Screening Job Applicants for Ethics: Can it be Done?" *ethikos* 20 no.3 (Nov./Dec. 2006): 8, 10; Mintz & Frost, "Transparency in Due-Diligence Background Checking: Setting a Standard," *ethikos* 18 no. 6 (May/June 2005): 5-6.)

148 **Debarment lists.** Check government debarment/exclusion lists for potential new hires. (See Jordan & Murphy, "Compliance Programs: What the Government Really Wants," *ACCA Docket* (July/Aug. 1996): 10, 19.)

149 **Background checks.** Check criminal conviction records of job applicants. Also consider checking other litigation records. (See Sherwood, "Screening Job Applicants for Ethics: Can it be Done?" *ethikos* 20 no. 8 (Nov./Dec. 2006): 10; Mintz & Frost, "Transparency in Due-Diligence Background Checking: Setting a Standard," *ethikos* 18 no. 6 (May/June 2005): 5, 6-7.)

150 **Checking officers.** Conduct periodic background checks on current officers in the company, no matter how long they have been with the company. (See Singer, "Tying Ethics to Evaluations at Nationwide Insurance Company," *ethikos* 21 no. 5 (Mar./Apr. 2008).)

151 **Ask your lawyer.** Consult with legal counsel on background checking to be sure you do not violate privacy laws.

152 **Promotion eligibility.** Have commitment to the compliance and ethics program and the company's code as a specific factor in determining eligibility for promotion. (See *Building Incentives in Your Compliance & Ethics Program* (Minneapolis: Society of Corporate Compliance and Ethics, 2007), http://www.corporatecompliance.org/Content/NavigationMenu/ Resources/IssuesAnswers/DRAFTwhitepaper-BuildingIncentivesCompliance_WOappdx.pdf.)

153 **Code to applicants.** Provide the company's code to those applying for positions in the company, with instructions that if they are not comfortable with what is in the code they should not proceed with applying to the company.

154 **Behavioral interviewing.** Consider using certain types of questions during job interviews that can give an indication of the interviewee's view of honesty and commitment to obeying the law. (See Sherwood, "Screening Job Applicants for Ethics: Can it be Done?" *ethikos* 20 no. 3 (Nov./Dec. 2006): 8, 9-10.)

155 **Third-party employee checks.** Require third parties doing work for the company to perform background checks on any of their employees doing such work.

156 **Annual reviews.** Have the chief compliance and ethics officer annually review the company's delegations of substantial discretionary authority and the systems in place to ensure those given authority meet the company's standards. (See Jordan & Murphy, "Compliance Programs: What the Government Really Wants," *ACCA Docket* (July/Aug. 1996): 10, 19.)

157 **Problematic new hires.** When potential new hires have troublesome elements in their backgrounds, require review and approval by the compliance and ethics officer before offering employment. (See Jordan & Murphy, "Compliance Programs: What the Government Really Wants," *ACCA Docket* (July/Aug. 1996): 10, 19.)

158 **Checking professionals.** Check licensing authorities and/or run checks for any disciplinary proceedings regarding a professional under consideration for hiring. (See Mintz & Frost, "Transparency in Due-Diligence Background Checking: Setting a Standard," *ethikos* 18 no. 6 (May/June 2005): 5, 7.)

G. USSGs item 4, training

Training is one of the most basic compliance and ethics tools, and is covered in USSGs item 4. Here are ideas to make training work.

159 **Learning from past mistakes.** Produce a training video covering actual compliance problems the company has experienced and what was learned from those experiences. (See Singer, "General Electric Company's True Confessions Ethics Video," *ethikos* 15 no. 2 (Sept./Oct. 2001): 5.)

160 **Mobile training.** Provide on-the-road training tools for traveling employees, such as interesting training CDs, or through compliance messages inserted into other company training CDs. (See Singer, "Coming This Season to KNTV: Marathon's Business Code of Conduct," *ethikos* 17 no. 3 (Nov./Dec. 2003): 9, 11.)

161 **Training from a newspaper.** Use a tool like an ethics newspaper, with newspaper-like features, as the centerpiece for a training session. The newspaper could include compliance and ethics case studies to be used in the training. (See Singer, "Ethics Training at Lockheed Martin Takes a Tabloid Turn," *ethikos* 15 no. 1 (July/Aug. 2001): 8.)

162 **TV format.** Model training on a TV show format, with a different online "program" (e.g., "Morning Report") for each risk area that is covered in the code of conduct. (See Singer, "Coming This Season to KNTV: Marathon's Business Code of Conduct," *ethikos* 17 no. 3 (Nov./Dec. 2003): 9.)

163 **Online training.** Use training formatted for Internet or intranet use; such online training allows companies to reach large numbers of employees in a short time frame, and to test their comprehension of the training. (See Murphy, "Internet's Speed, Efficiency Has Raised the Bar for Employee Compliance Training," *Prevention of Corporate Liability Current Report* 8 (Apr. 17, 2000): 32.)

164 **The right way.** In online, story-based training, after showing what someone has done wrong, also show an example of the right way to do things, so the message includes a positive element.

165 **Online training by working group.** Arrange the online training so the content varies based on what working group the employee is from. So a sales person's training would vary from a line manager's training, even when they were taking courses on the same risk area. (See Singer, "Coors Brewing Company's Ethics Code Training," *ethikos* 16 no. 2 (Sept./Oct. 2002): 4.)

166 **Case studies.** Use case studies based on actual company cases. These may include "near misses," to analyze mistakes and how to avoid similar breakdowns in the future. (See Frankcom, "Ssh, Ssh Don't Tell Me!" *ethikos* 21 no. 4 (Jan./Feb. 2008): 12; Kolasky, "Antitrust Compliance: The Government's Perspective," *ethikos* 16 no. 2 (Sept./Oct. 2002): 6-7.)

167 **Case study group feedback.** In case-study training, have small groups in the class give their analysis of the case, and other groups of colleagues in the class rate that group's approach. (See Singer, "Ethics Training at Lockheed Martin Takes a Tabloid Turn," *ethikos* 15 no. 1 (July/Aug. 2001): 8-9.)

168 **Flagging trouble.** In case study group sessions, give the participants red and green flags. As the case progresses, have participants wave the flag they think applies to signal whether conduct is acceptable or improper. (See Frankcom, "Ssh, Ssh Don't Tell Me!" *ethikos* 21 no. 4 (Jan./Feb. 2008): 12, 13.)

169 **"Scared straight."** Use a "scared straight" presentation by a convicted white-collar ex-felon relating how and why he or she got into trouble. The presenter offers a "just like me" example of what can go wrong. (See Kaplan, "Chapter 8: Corporate Lawbreakers as Sources of Interactive Training," in Sigler & Murphy, *Corporate Lawbreaking and Interactive Compliance*, (Westport, CT: Quorum Books, 1991).)

170 **Recognition certificate.** Provide a recognition certificate for those who have completed the compliance training. (See Murphy, "Job Aides, Toys or 'Tchatchkas': Getting the Compliance Message to Employees," *ethikos* 14 no. 5 (Mar./Apr. 2001): 8, 9-10.)

171 **Measure training's effectiveness.** Measure training using these steps: Test some employees before the training and then immediately after. Ninety days later, check again for retention and also for whether the training has caused the employees to change anything they do. (From Karen Wilson.)

172 **Feedback forms.** Have training attendees complete feedback forms, so you have input on what worked and what needs to be improved. (See Murphy, "Training 'in a Practical Manner,'" *Corporate Conduct Quarterly* (now *ethikos*) 6 (1998): 2, 6; Singer, "Coming This Season to KNTV: Marathon's Business Code of Conduct," *ethikos* 17 no. 3 (Nov./Dec. 2003): 9, 11; "App. 13-A: Antitrust Compliance Training Feedback," in Kaplan & Murphy, *Compliance Programs and the Corporate Sentencing Guidelines* (Eagan, MN: Thomson/West; 1993 & Ann'l Supp).)

173 **Orientation training.** Include compliance and ethics program coverage in new employee, manager and board training and orientation. (See Singer, "Caremark and Tenet's Prescription: 'Live' Ethics Training," *ethikos* 19 no.1 (July/Aug. 2005): 17-18.)

174 **Class competition.** Divide classes into small teams (e.g., 3-5 people) and create competition among the teams for answering questions correctly.

175 **Train the trainers.** Provide training on adult learning, public speaking and interactive training techniques for all those who present live compliance and ethics training. (See Murphy, "Training 'in a Practical Manner,'" *Corporate Conduct Quarterly* (now *ethikos*) 6 (1998): 2, 6.)

176 **Lawyers by phone.** When expert lawyers cannot provide or attend the training, they can be brought in by phone when appropriate to handle questions and emphasize key points. (See Murphy, "Training 'in a Practical Manner,'" *Corporate Conduct Quarterly* (now *ethikos*) 6 (1998): 2, 4.)

177 **Test it out.** When you have developed new live training, test it out first. For example, you might try delivering the training to a group from the compliance and ethics office for feedback. This lets you fine-tune the presentation and other techniques you may plan to use.

178 **Presentation pointers.** Provide a checklist of presentation pointers for all those doing live compliance training and presentations.

179 **Embedded training.** Embed relevant compliance and ethics messages within other management training programs and materials. (See Murphy, "Training 'in a Practical Manner,'" *Corporate Conduct Quarterly* (now *ethikos*) 6 (1998): 2, 6.)

180 **Mock files.** In live compliance training sessions, use a mock file of company documents and have participants identify compliance red flags embedded in the documents. This could also be done to train compliance auditors. (See Singer, "Granite Construction Adds 'Land Mines' to its Antitrust Compliance Training," *ethikos* 18 no. 6 (May/June 2005): 15.)

181 **Supervisors' guide.** Develop a compliance and ethics discussion or facilitator's guide for supervisors to cover compliance topics effectively at staff meetings. This could also include videos. (See Singer, "General Electric Company's True Confessions Ethics Video," *ethikos* 15 no. 2 (Sept./Oct. 2001): 5, 9-10.)

182 **Role of supervisors.** Add into the standard compliance and ethics training some features focused on the additional role of supervisors, such as their responsibility to respond to subordinates' compliance questions. (See Singer, "Honda's Ethics Training Shifts to a Higher Gear," *ethikos* 13 no. 4 (Jan./Feb. 2000): 6.)

183 **Computer kiosks.** For computer-based training for assembly line employees, consider setting up computer kiosks to allow employees to take the training while minimizing time and disruption. (See Singer, "Honda's Ethics Training Shifts to a Higher Gear," *ethikos* 13 no. 4 (Jan./Feb. 2000): 6, 8.)

184 **Audience response systems.** In live training, use wireless keypads to obtain attendees' input and make the session more interactive. (See Singer, "Caremark and Tenet's Prescription: 'Live' Ethics Training," *ethikos* 19 no. 1 (July/Aug. 2005): 7.)

185 **Training prerequisite.** Make compliance training a prerequisite for certain high-risk jobs. If there is already required training for a position, include coverage of related compliance issues, and test for comprehension. (See Sigler & Murphy, *Interactive Corporate Compliance: An Alternative to Regulatory Compulsion* (Westport, CT: Quorum Books, 1988): 87.; Sharon Taylor.)

186 **E-mail reminders.** Use an escalating series of e-mails to remind employees that they have missed required training. Have supervisors and officers copied as the e-mails escalate in urgency.

187 **Audit follow-up.** When business units fall short of their compliance training goals, or a senior leader in the unit falls short, have that unit included in the priority list for compliance auditing. This tactic both reflects increased risk in that unit, and serves as a deterrent for missing the training.

188 **Foreign lawyers' presentations.** In compliance presentations outside your home country, include a presentation by a local lawyer about that country's similar legal requirements.

189 **Simultaneous translations.** For compliance presentations that are to be simultaneously translated for employees who speak another language, provide advance information to the translators, such as copies of your notes, PowerPoints, and background materials, to assist them in accurately translating your presentation.

190 **Commercially produced videos.** Commercially available training videos using dramatic stories can serve as a supplement to live training. They can also set a consistent, base level of training when used by different instructors. (See Murphy, "Training 'in a Practical Manner,'" *Corporate Conduct Quarterly* (now ethikos) 6 (1998): 2, 4.)

191 **Customized videos.** Customized videos can include messages from the CEO and compliance officer, and address unique company circumstances, but need to be done at a professional level to be effective. (See Murphy, "Training 'in a Practical Manner,'" *Corporate Conduct Quarterly* (now *ethikos*) 6 (1998): 2, 4-5.)

192 **Playing games.** Use the equivalent of a board game to cover the key compliance messages. Senior managers can act as judges to debate why certain answers are right or wrong. (See Murphy, "New Ideas for Managing Business Ethics and Legal Compliance," *The Journal of Commerce & Finance* (Villanova University) 8 (Fall 1991): 11, 12.)

193 **Team agreements.** At the start of a live training session, develop a "team agreement" with the class, posted on a board visible to the class. The agreement can include the objectives of the training, and how all will participate, based on input from the group. (See Murphy, "Training 'in a Practical Manner,'" *Corporate Conduct Quarterly* (now *ethikos*) 6 (1998): 2, 3.)

194 **Just-in-time training.** Arrange training to be provided just at the point an employee needs it. For example, if a company requires employees to get approval to attend a trade association, a training program could be designed to be completed online as part of the approval process. (See Murphy, "Training 'in a Practical Manner,'" *Corporate Conduct Quarterly* (now *ethikos*) 6 (1998): 2, 5-6.)

195 **Oral tests.** In live training, after the presentation the instructor can go around the room asking questions. This technique can be described as a "test of the instructor," because at this point if the students missed something it means the instructor didn't explain it well enough. This also surfaces misunderstandings by the students at a point when they can be fixed. (See Murphy, "Training 'in a Practical Manner,'" *Corporate Conduct Quarterly* (now ethikos) 6 (1998): 2, 4.)

196 **Role playing.** In live training, having employees take on such roles as lawyer, competitor, customer, prosecutor, etc., can allow them to experience the actual compliance risks covered in the training. (See Murphy, "Training 'in a Practical Manner,'" *Corporate Conduct Quarterly* (now *ethikos*) 6 (1998): 2, 3; Sigler & Murphy, *Interactive Corporate Compliance: An Alternative to Regulatory Compulsion* (Westport, CT: Quorum Books, 1988): 86.)

197 **Small groups.** Train employees, at least those in the highest risk groups, in small group sessions, which allows for more interaction. (See Singer, "Learning from the Salt Lake City Olympics Scandal," *ethikos* 14 no. 5 (Mar./Apr. 2001): 1, 3.)

198 **Q&A sessions.** At the end of live training, allow time for questions and answers and have a subject-matter expert available to respond. (See Sigler & Murphy, *Interactive Corporate Compliance: An Alternative to Regulatory Compulsion* (Westport, CT: Quorum Books, 1988): 85.)

199 **Cascading training.** Managers may be trained and then be asked to conduct the compliance and ethics training for their own subordinates, so that they lead by example and because subordinates may respond better to training by their own supervisors. This training may then be audited to determine how effective the managers were. (See Kaplan, "The Tone at the Middle," *ethikos* 20 no. 2 (Sept./Oct. 2006): 5, 7.)

200 **Supervisors' certification.** Require supervisors to certify that all of their subordinates have completed required compliance training, and have each layer of management above do the same, with the CEO ultimately certifying completion of the training to the board. (See Jordan & Murphy, "Compliance Programs: What the Government Really Wants," *ACCA Docket* (July/Aug. 1996): 10, 24.)

201 **Training introductions.** Have executives and other senior managers take the time to give an in-person introductory statement at the beginning of important compliance and ethics training sessions. (See Singer, "Caremark and Tenet's Prescription: 'Live' Ethics Training," *ethikos* 19 no. 1 (July/Aug. 2005): 17-18.)

202 **Tips for live training.** Be sure the facility is comfortable, all the equipment is working, there are no distractions, refreshments are provided, and the presenter is effective and has practiced.

203 **Minimum training hours.** Set a minimum number of compliance and ethics training hours per year for employees, based on their job responsibilities and risks. (See HHS, "OIG Compliance Program Guidance for Pharmaceutical Manufacturers," *Federal Register* 68 (May 5, 2003): 23,731, 23,740.)

204 **Managers' follow-ups.** Require supervisors who attend the compliance training to report back within a stated time on steps they have taken to assure understanding of and compliance with the compliance message by their subordinates. (See Sigler & Murphy, *Interactive Corporate Compliance: An Alternative to Regulatory Compulsion* (Westport, CT: Quorum Books, 1988): 93.)

205 **Managers Boot Camp.** Provide intensive, one- to two-day compliance and ethics training sessions for managers, covering a broad range of compliance risks that apply to them. (See Singer, "Sun Microsystems Sends Managers to Fiduciary Boot Camp," *ethikos* 16 no. 5 (Mar./April 2003): 8.)

H. USSGs item 4, other communications tools

Training is not the only way to reach those who act for the company, and it is only part of USSGs item 4. Following are other ways to reach out with the compliance and ethics message.

206 **Communications plan.** Develop an annual communications plan for the compliance program to get the message out on an ongoing and consistent basis. (See Murphy & Swenson, "20 Questions to Ask About Your Code of Conduct," *ethikos* 17 no. 1 (July/Aug. 2003): 7, 9.)

207 **Inventory.** Inventory all the company and business unit newsletters, magazines, email broadcast systems, Web sites and other communications media and include these in the compliance communications plan.

208 **Web site.** Have a compliance program Web site with useful resources for employees and others. (See Singer, "Raytheon's Gratuities and Gifts Policy Has Some Give," *ethikos* 15 no. 4 (Jan./Feb. 2002): 4, 6; Singer, "At Bellsouth, the Main Ethics Website is the Internal One," *ethikos* 14 no.4 (Jan./Feb. 2001): 8.)

209 **"What would you do?"** On the compliance and ethics intranet site, have a "what would you do" section, featuring an employee question and soliciting employee input. The management solution could then be added after the input was received. (See Singer, "At Bellsouth, the Main Ethics Website is the Internal One," *ethikos* 14 no. 4 (Jan./Feb. 2001): 8 9.)

210 **Ethics in the news.** The intranet site can feature outside news stories about other companies' ethics and compliance problems, for employees to learn from others' mistakes. (See Singer, "At Bellsouth, the Main Ethics Website is the Internal One," *ethikos* 14 no. 4 (Jan./Feb. 2001): 8, 9.)

211 **Government compliance guides.** Some government agencies provide brief guides to explain what the relevant laws require. You might be able to obtain these to assist in your compliance communications for employees and agents.

212 **Job offer letters.** Include a reference to the code of conduct in any new-employee offering or hiring letter. This helps assure that new people start with an understanding of the importance of compliance and ethics at the company.

213 **Employment contracts.** Add adherence to the code of conduct as a condition in any employment contracts.

214 **Paycheck inserts.** Use paycheck inserts to emphasize the code of conduct and/or publicize the helpline and compliance Web site.

215 **Publicize disciplinary cases.** Publicize disciplinary cases from within the company as practical learning opportunities. (See Singer, "Dupont's Daring Communications Formula," *ethikos* 17 no.4 (Jan/Feb 2004): 1; Murphy & McCollum, "Communicating 'in a Practical Manner:' Bell Atlantic's Report on Integrity," *Corporate Conduct Quarterly* (now *ethikos*) 4 (1996): 59; Singer, "Boeing Company's Ethics Improvements Take Flight," *ethikos* 20 no. 1 (July/Aug. 2006): 5, 6.)

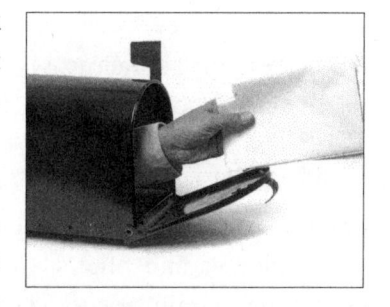

216 **Weekly C&E column.** Have a weekly column in the company newsletter from the compliance officer. (See Prachar, "Waste Management's 'Core Values,'" *ethikos* 21 no. 3 (Nov./Dec. 2007): 7.)

217 **"You be the judge."** Include a compliance/ethics "you be the judge" feature in a company newsletter. This gives employees a practical problem and asks them to develop a solution. The answer can then be provided elsewhere in the newsletter or on a Web site. (See Murphy & McCollum, "Communicating 'in a Practical Manner:' Bell Atlantic's Report on Integrity," *Corporate Conduct Quarterly* (now *ethikos*) 4 (1996): 59, 66-67.)

218 **C&E newsletter.** Have a separate compliance and ethics newsletter, which can include interesting case studies. (See Murphy & McCollum, "Communicating 'in a Practical Manner:' Bell Atlantic's Report on Integrity," *Corporate Conduct Quarterly* (now *ethikos*) 4 (1996): 59.)

219 **Branding the program.** Develop a "branding" strategy for the program. This can be used on all program materials, to help convey a consistent, coordinated message. One branding symbol companies have used is a lighthouse. In this sense the compliance and ethics program is a guiding light. (See Murphy & McCollum, "Communicating 'in a Practical Manner': Bell Atlantic's Report on Integrity," *Corporate Conduct Quarterly* (now *ethikos*) 4 (1996): 59; See Singer, "Marsh's Business Reforms: Much Ground Covered in Little Time," *ethikos* 19 no. 6 (May/June 2006): 1, 3.)

220 **Compliance manuals.** Use compliance manuals in the compliance risk areas, such as antitrust. (See Murphy, "Compliance Guidance From the United Kingdom," *ethikos* 20 no. 5 (Mar./Apr. 2007), foreign bribery and government contracting.)

221 **Dos and don'ts.** Provide a list of *dos* and *don'ts* in the compliance risk areas. These could be done on laminated pocket cards. (See Sigler & Murphy, *Interactive Corporate Compliance: An Alternative to Regulatory Compulsion* (Westport, CT: Quorum Books, 1988): 85.)

222 **Best ideas contest.** Have a contest throughout the company for the best compliance and ethics communications ideas. (See Boehme, "How BP Communicates Integrity: Creative Engagement to Win Hearts and Minds," *ethikos* 19 no. 5 (Mar./Apr. 2006): 1, 3.)

223 **Knowledge contests.** Have contests among different departments to see which department has the best knowledge of ethics and compliance. (See Singer, "TAP Pharma Isn't Afraid to Show 'a Little Levity,'" *ethikos* 19 no.5 (Mar./Apr. 2006): 16.)

224 **Posters.** Use posters asking an interesting compliance question and giving the page in the Code, or the location on the compliance and ethics Web site, where the answer can be found. (See Boehme, "How BP Communicates Integrity: Creative Engagement to Win Hearts and Minds," *ethikos* 19 no. 5 (Mar./Apr. 2006): 1, 2.)

225 **Telecommuters.** If there are telecommuting employees, include coverage of compliance and ethics and of the code in any telecommuting agreements. (See Berg, "Ethics and the Inclusion of the Virtual Workforce," *ethikos* 14 no. 2 (Sept./Oct. 2000): 7, 9.)

226 **Tchotchkes.** Consider job aides and promotional items to promote the program and such features as the Web site and helpline. There is a very broad variety of these items, ranging from coasters to hats, to calendars. (See Murphy, "Job Aides, Toys or 'Tchatchkas': Getting the Compliance Message to Employees," *ethikos* 14 no.5 (Mar./Apr. 2001): 8; Kaplan & Murphy, "App. 8-S: Compliance Job Aids," in *Compliance Programs and the Corporate Sentencing Guidelines* (Eagan, MN: Thomson/West; 1993 & Ann'l Supp).)

227 **E-mail newsletters.** Provide an e-mail newsletter with current compliance events, answers to common questions, etc. (See Zinn, "*ComplianceGrams:* A Case Study in Communicating and Teaching Compliance," *Corporate Conduct Quarterly* (now *ethikos*) 4 (1995): 1.)

228 **Management directives.** Send management directives from senior line managers to employees covering key compliance areas and the company's related compliance policy. These can be posted where employees will see them. (See Jordan & Murphy, "Compliance Programs: What the Government Really Wants," *ACCA Docket* (July/Aug. 1996): 10, 20; *Reich v. Food Lion*, no. 4:93CV457 (M.D.N.C., Aug. 3, 1993).)

229 **Online games.** Provide an ethics/compliance game online to cover key compliance points in an interesting way. (See Boehme, "How BP Communicates Integrity: Creative Engagement to Win Hearts and Minds," *ethikos* 19 no. 5 (Mar./Apr. 2006): 1 2-3.)

230 **Audio conferences.** Have audio conferences where employees can call in with questions about compliance and ethics issues. (See Singer, "TAP Pharma Isn't Afraid to Show 'a Little Levity,'" *ethikos* 19 no.5, (Mar./Apr. 2006): 16-17.)

231 **Calendars.** Issue calendars with a different compliance and ethics message on each day or month. (See Murphy, "Job Aides, Toys or 'Tchatchkas': Getting the Compliance Message to Employees," *ethikos* 14 no. 5 (Mar./Apr. 2001): 8, 10.)

232 **Compliance and ethics puzzles.** Include a compliance and ethics related crossword puzzle or word search in your company's newsletter. Completed submissions of the puzzle/answers can be submitted for a drawing to win a prize (where such drawings are legal, of course.) (From Doug Beeuwsaert.)

I. USSGs item 5, helplines, reporting systems, preventing retaliation

Compliance and ethics programs need a way to allow employees and others to raise questions and obtain advice. It is also essential that the company prohibit retaliation. These aspects of a program are part of item 5 of the USSGs.

233 **Anonymous caller call-backs.** Ask anonymous callers to call back at set time intervals so they can get progress reports on their calls, and respond to requests for additional information. (See "How United Technologies' Board Meets its Compliance Obligations," *ethikos* 11 no. 1 (July/Aug. 1997): 4-5.)

234 **Employee training.** Include coverage of the helpline system and non-retaliation policy in employee training, to increase awareness of and confidence in the reporting system. (See Martens & Crowell, "Whistleblowing: A Global Perspective (Part II)," *ethikos* 16 no. 1 (July/Aug. 2002): 9-10.)

235 **Testing it first.** Before launching a helpline or other reporting system, you can test it out in one business unit first. (See Murphy, "Hotlines, an Overview," *Corporate Conduct Quarterly* (now *ethikos*) 4 (1995): 7, 10.)

236 **Ombuds office.** Use a neutral ombuds office to surface issues people might otherwise be afraid to raise. (See Singer, "Ombuds office Helps Coca-Cola Bottler Avoid Explosions," *ethikos* 19 no. 3 (Nov/Dec 2005): 11; Singer, "Alliance-Bernstein Invests in New Ombuds office," *ethikos* 19 no. 6 (May/June 2006): 12.)

237   **Location.** For an ombuds office or other confidential source that employees can go to for advice and assistance, place the person's office where employees can approach without being noticed, such as a floor with conference rooms. Also, allow meetings to be arranged off site. (See Singer, "Alliance-Bernstein Invests in New Ombuds office, *ethikos* 19 no. 6 (May/June 2006): 12-13.)

238   **Ombuds report.** Provide an annual report by the ombuds office to all employees, explaining what the office does. (See Singer, "Do You Know Me? I'm the American Express Ombudsperson....," *ethikos* 19 no. 2 (Sept./Oct. 2005): 12, 13.)

239   **Ombuds independence.** Ensure the ombuds' independence by using an employment contract and having the ombuds report to the CEO with the ability to report to the audit committee as well. (See Singer, "Do You Know Me? I'm the American Express Ombudsperson....," *ethikos* 19 no. 2 (Sept./Oct. 2005): 12, 14.)

240   **Ombuds data.** Use the ombuds' office case data and trends as a guide for what is happening in the company. (See Redmond & Williams, "The Organizational Ombuds: Complementing the Ethics office," *ethikos* 17 no. 2 (Sept./Oct. 2003): 10.)

241   **Call-back times.** Give helpline callers a set call-back time and a case number for a status report or resolution, and in case investigators have more questions. (See Singer, "Bracing for Deregulation, AEP Boosts Ethics Training," *ethikos* 11 no. 1 (July/Aug. 1997): 1, 3; Singer, "Exelon Excels at Reaching Out," *ethikos* 16 no. 6 (May/June 2003): 7, 8.)

242   **Web-based helpline.** Use an online or Web-based helpline system as an adjunct to the telephone line.

243 **Helpline.** Call the line a helpline, rather than the harsher sounding "hotline," and make it clear that the line provides advice and not just a reporting outlet. (See Murphy, "Hotlines, an Overview," *Corporate Conduct Quarterly* (now *ethikos*) 4 (1995): 7, 8; "The Conference Board Benchmarks Ethics and Compliance Programs," *ethikos* 20 no. 3 (Nov./Dec. 2006): 14, 15; Singer, "Developing *Effective* Helplines: Shell Oil and Lubrizol," *ethikos* 19 no. 2 (Sept./Oct. 2005): 5.)

244 **Customer complaint lines.** Monitor customer service/complaint lines for indications of consumer protection and product safety concerns. (See Sharpe, "The Value of a Complaints System in Effective Legal Compliance Systems," *ethikos* 18 no. 3 (Nov/Dec 2004): 11.)

245 **E-mail box.** Consider an e-mail box or a reporting form that can be downloaded from the company's intranet site and mailed in to report concerns. (See Singer, "Aventis' Helpline: Translating from the Urdu (et al.)," *ethikos* 17 no.3 (Nov./Dec. 2003): 4.)

246 **Open door.** Have an open door policy among managers that welcomes employee comments and concerns. This may require training for managers so they know how to respond to employees. (See HHS, "OIG Compliance Program Guidance for Pharmaceutical Manufacturers," *Federal Register* 68 (May 5, 2003): 23,731, 23,741.)

247 **Showing the flag.** Have those who handle helpline calls for the company make presentations to employees throughout the company, so employees feel comfortable knowing what happens if they call the helpline. (See Martens & Crowell, "Whistleblowing: A Global Perspective (Part II)," *ethikos* 16 no. 1(July/Aug. 2002): 9, 11.)

248 **Publicity.** Publicize the helpline through such vehicles as the code, posters, handout cards, brochures, telephone stickers, and tchotchkes. (See Murphy, "Hotlines, an Overview," *Corporate Conduct Quarterly* (now *ethikos*) 4 (1995): 7, 9; Singer, "Developing *Effective* Helplines: Shell Oil and Lubrizol," *ethikos* 19 no. 2 (Sept./Oct. 2005): 5, 7.)

249 **Legal review.** To be sure that calls were appropriately handled, you can have a lawyer review the helpline call records periodically to spot any legal issues that might have been missed. (See Murphy, "Hotlines, an Overview," *Corporate Conduct Quarterly* (now *ethikos*) 4 (1995): 7, 9.)

250 **Non-retaliation outreach.** Have a periodic follow-up/call back system to check for possible retaliation against those who have used the helpline or otherwise raised compliance concerns. (See Murphy, "Hotlines, an Overview," *Corporate Conduct Quarterly* (now *ethikos*) 4 (1995): 7, 9; Singer, "Waste Management's Helpline Use is No Longer 'off the Charts,'" *ethikos* 16 no. 1 (July/Aug. 2002): 5 12.)

251 **No caller ID.** If the helpline is handled internally, make sure there is no caller ID and that employees know this. (See Murphy, "Hotlines, an Overview," *Corporate Conduct Quarterly* (now *ethikos*) 4 (1995): 7, 9; Singer, "Developing *Effective* Helplines: Shell Oil and Lubrizol," *ethikos* 19 no. 2 (Sept./Oct. 2005): 5, 7.)

252 **Test calls.** Place occasional test calls to the helpline to test out its timeliness and effectiveness.

253 **Database.** Have a centralized database of the helpline calls and investigations. This allows analysis to ensure consistency. (See Muse, "Hotlines Must Adapt to an Ever-Changing Global Environment," 20 *ethikos* no.11 (Jan./Feb. 2007).)

254 **Feedback.** Give callers feedback, such as an idea of what investigative steps were taken and whether any corrective actions were warranted. (See Murphy, "Hotlines, an Overview," *Corporate Conduct Quarterly* (now *ethikos*) 4 (1995): 7, 9; Martens & Crowell, "Whistleblowing: A Global Perspective (Part II)," *ethikos* 16 no. 1 (July/Aug. 2002): 9, 11.)

255 **Outsourcing.** Use a third party service to answer helplines, to ensure 24-hour coverage and help protect anonymity. (See Singer, "Developing *Effective* Helplines: Shell Oil and Lubrizol," *ethikos* 19 no. 2 (Sept./Oct. 2005): 5-6.)

256 **Training supervisors.** Train supervisors on how to respond to subordinates' complaints and concerns when expressed to the supervisors, and emphasize the importance of the non-retaliation policy. (See Kaplan, "The Tone at the Middle," *ethikos* 20 no. 2(Sept./Oct. 2006): 5, 7; Singer, "Creating an Open, Non-Retaliatory Workplace," *ethikos* 19 no. 5 (Mar./Apr. 2006): 4, 5.)

257 **Encouraging callers.** Communicate to employees that calls made in good faith are encouraged, and that "good faith" means that the employee believes something is true, even if it later turns out not to be so. (See Singer, "Creating an Open, Non-Retaliatory Workplace," *ethikos* 19 no. 5 (Mar./Apr. 2006): 4.)

258 **Call records.** Keep a record not just of complaint calls, but also of calls for advice. Both types of calls show the reporting system is working.

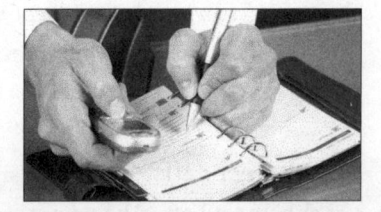

259 **Prioritizing calls.** Have a system for prioritizing calls, such as "urgent," "serious" and "routine." (See Singer, "Developing *Effective* Helplines: Shell Oil and Lubrizol," *ethikos* 19 no. 2 (Sept./Oct. 2005): 5, 6.)

260 **Benchmarking.** Measure the impact of your reporting system by comparing the percentage of your employee base who use the system, to numbers at peer companies. (See Petry, "Assessing Corporate Culture: Part II," *ethikos* 19 no. 1 (July/Aug. 2005): 10, 13.)

261 **Local contacts.** In the various business units and locations have compliance and ethics people designated to handle concerns and questions. They can serve as a communications liaison. (See Martens & Crowell, "Whistleblowing: A Global Perspective (Part II)," *ethikos* 16 no. 1 (July/Aug. 2002): 9, 11.)

J. USSGs item 5, compliance audits

Auditing is a key way of enforcing and checking on the success of any compliance mandate. These ideas cover the audit point in item 5 of the USSGs.

262 **Unannounced audits.** Conduct unannounced compliance audits, not just those that are announced. This would be part of auditing to "detect criminal conduct" in the words of the Sentencing Guidelines. (See Roberts, "Antitrust Compliance Programs Under the Guidelines: Initial Observations From the Government's Viewpoint," *Corporate Conduct Quarterly* (now *ethikos*) 2 (Summer 1992): 1, 2; Kolasky, "Antitrust Compliance: The Government's Perspective," *ethikos* 16 no. 2 (Sept./Oct. 2002): 6, 8.)

263 **Internal audit.** Have the internal audit organization conduct audits of the operation of the compliance program, and of substantive compliance in the company's operations. (See Jordan & Murphy, "Compliance Programs: What the Government Really Wants," *ACCA Docket* (July/Aug. 1996): 10, 26; Singer, "Shell Oil Company 'Energizes' its Ethics Commitment," *ethikos* 16 no. 3 (Nov./Dec. 2002): 8, 13.)

264 **Train internal auditors.** Train the internal auditors on the key compliance risk areas, including red flags to look for. This increases their ability to detect violations, even in routine audits. Emphasize that they should refer all legal issues to counsel immediately.

265 **Manual for auditors.** Provide a practical manual for internal auditors identifying compliance red flags in the various risk areas.

266 **Internal audit charter.** Include compliance responsibilities in the charter for the internal audit organization.

267   **Piggybacking.** Have compliance and ethics questions and checks added into standard audits by the internal audit organization. (See Singer, "How Xerox Weaves Ethics Into the Internal Audit Process," *ethikos* 20 no. 5 (Mar./Apr. 2007): 11.)

268   **Desk audits.** Conduct "desk audits" where auditors review high-risk employees' files for compliance red flags. (See Singer, "Audits Reduce Compliance Risk at United Technologies," *ethikos* 14 no. 5 (Mar./Apr. 2001): 12.)

269   **Pre-audit meetings.** Hold pre-audit meetings with those who will be subject to a compliance audit, to explain what the audit is about and why it is being done. This can reduce anxiety about the audit and facilitate the process.

270   **Publicize audits.** Publicize your compliance audits, to serve as a deterrent. (See Murphy, "Compliance Guidance From the United Kingdom," *ethikos* 20 no. 5 (Mar./Apr. 2007): 5, 6.)

271   **Deep dives.** Conduct full-scale, management deep dives—intensive, on-site reviews of a business segment to reach beyond conventional audits—for compliance purposes. (See Murphy, "The Measurement Challenge (Part I): Introducing the Deep Dive," *ethikos* 17, no. 5 (May/June 2004): 7; "The Measurement Challenge (Part II): Implementing the 'Deep Dive,'" *ethikos* 18 no.1 (July/Aug 2004): 11; "The Measurement Challenge (Part III): Results from the 'Deep Dive,'" *ethikos* 18 no. 2 (Sept./Oct. 2004): 11.)

272   **Inventory of checking techniques.** Develop an inventory of auditing, monitoring and checking techniques, to be applied to the different risks based on the risk assessment. (See "App. 13-C: Inventory of Audit and Monitoring Tools," in Kaplan & Murphy, *Compliance Programs and the Corporate Sentencing Guidelines* (Eagan, MN: Thomson/West; 1993 & Ann'l Supp).)

273 **C&E audit plans.** Develop an annual compliance and ethics audit plan, based on the risk assessment. This could draw on all the audit and assessment tools developed for each risk area.

274 **Vendor audits.** Conduct vendor audits, including surveys on compliance matters relating to the vendor's dealings with the company. (See Singer, "Audits Reduce Compliance Risk at United Technologies," *ethikos* 14 no. 5 (Mar./Apr. 2001): 12.)

275 **Finding best practices.** Include within the scope of compliance audits and deep dives instructions to look for best practices and good examples to share with the rest of the company, so that these reviews are not viewed solely as negative. (See Murphy, "The Measurement Challenge (Part III): Results from the 'Deep Dive,'" *ethikos* 18 no.2 (Sept./Oct. 2004): 11.)

276 **Follow-ups.** Have a system for monitoring all findings and recommendations in compliance audits, to ensure that problems are fixed. This technique can call for a project management process.

277 **Meet and exchange.** Have the compliance and ethics group and internal audit meet periodically to exchange experiences and findings. (See Singer, "How Xerox Weaves Ethics Into the Internal Audit Process," *ethikos* 20 no. 5 (Mar./Apr. 2007): 11, 12.)

278 **Open-ended questions.** Have compliance auditors end each interview with an open-ended question, such as "is there anything else I should have asked you or anything else I should know?" This gives employees a chance to raise compliance and ethics concerns even if they were outside the scope of the audit. (See Murphy, "I've Been Waiting for You to Call," *ethikos* 19 no. 6 (May/June 2006): 15, 16.)

279 **Talk to assistants.** When conducting audits and reviews of senior managers, also include their assistants. (See Kolasky, "Antitrust Compliance: The Government's Perspective," *ethikos* 16 no. 2 (Sept./Oct. 2002): 6, 13.)

K. USSGs item 5, other types of checking systems, monitoring techniques, and program evaluations

Audits are not the only way to check on how a compliance and ethics program is working. The ideas below cover the broader range of points covered under USSGs item 5.

280 **Exit interviews.** Include questions about the program and possible violations in exit interviews. Exit interviews could also be conducted by phone or through a Web site. (See Sherwood, "The Exit Interview: A Final Compliance Check," *ethikos* 18 no.6 (May/June 2005): 13, 14; HHS, "OIG Compliance Program Guidance for Pharmaceutical Manufacturers," *Federal Register* 68 (May 5, 2003): 23,731, 23,741.)

281 **Third-party exit interviews.** To protect anonymity and to encourage candor, use a third party to conduct exit interviews. (See Sherwood, "The Exit Interview: A Final Compliance Check," *ethikos* 18 no. 6 (May/June 2005): 13, 14.)

282 **Walk-arounds.** Do site "walk arounds" to check for things like required compliance posters (e.g., EEO, safety, etc.), objectionable pictures, safety hazards, etc. (See Kaplan, "Compliance Programs for Smaller Companies," *ethikos* 21 no. 4 (Jan./Feb. 2008): 6, 8; *U.S. Sentencing Guidelines*, Section 8B2.1, Commentary Note 2(C)(iii).)

283 **Employee surveys.** Use employee surveys to gauge employee awareness of the compliance and ethics program and their views of its effectiveness. (See "Sara Lee Corporation Relies on its Business Practices Officers Overseas," *ethikos* 11 no. 3 (Nov./Dec. 1997): 4; Singer, "How Xerox Weaves Ethics Into the Internal Audit Process," *ethikos* 20 no. 5 (Mar./Apr. 2007): 11, 12.)

284 **Survey piggybacking.** If you cannot get a separate survey on compliance and ethics, piggyback a few compliance and ethics questions on an existing employee survey. (See Petry, "Assessing Corporate Culture: Part II," *ethikos* 19 no. 1(July/Aug. 2005): 10.)

285 **Employee focus groups.** Use employee focus groups for deeper insights into employee compliance concerns and views about the effectiveness of the compliance and ethics program.

286 **High-tech feedback sessions.** Use high-tech group sessions, with instant voting and feedback techniques, to determine the impact of the program and employees' views on ethics at the company. (See Singer, "AEP's Ethics Interviews Are 'About the Passion of the People,'" *ethikos* 13 no. 6 (May/June 2000): 1, 3.)

287 **Employee interviews.** Interview random samples of employees, individually and in groups, to probe the effectiveness of the compliance and ethics program and employees' perceptions of ethics in the company. (See Singer, "AEP's Ethics Interviews Are 'About the Passion of the People,'" *ethikos* 13 no.6 (May/June 2000): 1.)

288 **Third-party surveys.** Use surveys of third parties to assess their views of the company's ethics and commitment to compliance. This can include former employees, competitors, suppliers and consumers. (See Petry, "Assessing Corporate Culture," *ethikos* 18 no. 5 (Mar./Apr. 2005): 1, 3; Singer, "Is a Company Ethical? Just Ask the Competition," *ethikos* 16 no. 3 (Nov./Dec. 2002): 1.)

289 **Evaluations to the board.** Have those who review and evaluate the program provide their reports directly to the board, rather than to those being evaluated. This helps ensure objectivity in the report.

290 **Subject matter program reviews.** Conduct separate assessments of compliance and ethics program efforts in each risk area, not just the overall program. This is common in such areas as environmental compliance and workplace safety, but can be done in all risk areas, including antitrust, harassment, foreign bribery, etc. (See Kaplan, "Risk-Based Compliance Program Management," *ethikos* 19 no. 5 (Mar./Apr. 2006): 7, 9.)

291 **Peer reviews.** Consider peer reviews of the program with other companies, modeled after the approach taken in academia. (See Crawford, "Using Peer Reviews to Assess Your Compliance Program," *ethikos* 18 no. 5(Mar./Apr. 2005): 12.)

292 **Questionnaires.** Require employees/managers in sensitive positions to complete periodic questionnaires identifying compliance issues and questions they may have, such as conflicts of interest.

293 **Self-assessment guides.** Provide managers with a set of compliance self-assessment guides, checklists, kits, lists of red flags, etc. Have managers/employees complete a detailed compliance checklist of key risk areas, indicating if they are in compliance with each point. This can guide supervisors in overseeing compliance among their subordinates, and also help to educate those involved on the risk areas covered.

294 **Business unit self-assessments.** Require business units to complete annual self-assessments, evaluating their own success in compliance program functions such as distribution of helpline posters and promoting awareness of the code, and substantive risk areas such as conflicts of interest and antitrust compliance. (See Singer, "How TRW's Legal and Ethics Compliance is Reviewed Annually," *ethikos* 15 no. 2 (Sept./Oct. 2001): 7; Singer, "Shell Oil Company 'Energizes' its Ethics Commitment," *ethikos* 16 no. 3 (Nov./Dec. 2002): 8, 12.)

295 **Business unit self-monitoring.** Provide the business units with protocols and checklists for them to use in developing their own compliance self-monitoring plans. These could be placed on the company intranet, and be based on the same factors company auditors would use in conducting compliance reviews. (See Singer, "Southern Company Sets Sights on Self-Monitoring," *ethikos* 14 no.2 (Sept./Oct. 2000): 12.)

296 **Check self-assessments.** When management self-assessments are used, conduct some audits or checks of the self-assessments and hold those who were not honest accountable. (See Singer, "How TRW's Legal and Ethics Compliance is Reviewed Annually," *ethikos* 15 no. 2 (Sept./Oct. 2001): 7, 8.)

297 **Mystery shoppers.** Consider the use of testers, such as mystery shoppers, to test compliance performance, e.g., in such risk areas as consumer protection and consumer discrimination.

298 **Responsibility for monitoring.** Include responsibility for compliance and ethics monitoring in the position descriptions and evaluations of all managers. (See Murphy, "When Starting Your Compliance Program, Survey What's Already in Place—and in Practice," *ethikos* 16 no. 5 (Mar./Apr. 2003): 5, 7).

299 **Lawyers as monitors.** Include in the position descriptions of corporate lawyers and in the law department's charter that the lawyers' role includes monitoring compliance. Thus, each time a lawyer participates in a meeting he or she is functioning as part of the compliance monitoring process. (See Kolasky, "Antitrust Compliance: The Government's Perspective," *ethikos* 16 no. 2(Sept./Oct. 2002): 6, 8.)

300 **Monitoring field sales practices.** Conduct management ride-alongs and random spot checks of sales people to monitor their selling practices. (See HHS, "OIG Compliance Program Guidance for Pharmaceutical Manufacturers," *Federal Register* 68 (May 5, 2003): 23,731, 23,739.)

301 **Field training as monitoring.** Consider small-group live training exercises at field locations as a form of compliance monitoring. Question and answer sessions after the training allow an experienced trainer to gain a sense of what is happening at that location. (See Sigler & Murphy, *Interactive Corporate Compliance: An Alternative to Regulatory Compulsion* (Westport, CT: Quorum Books, 1988): 83-84, 86; Murphy, "Testing Out," *ethikos* 21 no. 4 (Jan./Feb. 2008): 9, 10.)

302 **Levels of assessment.** Evaluate your program on three levels: design, implementation and impact. (See Swenson, Avelino & Ben-Chorin, "Chapter 18: Measuring the Effectiveness of Compliance and Ethics Programs," in Kaplan & Murphy, *Compliance Programs and the Corporate Sentencing Guidelines* (Eagan, MN: Thomson/West; 1993 & Ann'l Supp).)

303 **Outside reviews.** Have an outside firm with compliance and ethics expertise conduct an independent review and assessment of the company's overall compliance and ethics program. The final report could go directly to the board.

304 **Internal audit review for the board.** Have the internal audit department review the compliance and ethics program and report separately to the board on its findings. (See Daly, "Ethics Programs and the Changes in the Boardroom," *ethikos* 14 no. 2 (Sept./Oct. 2000): 4, 6.)

305 **Measuring subcultures.** In measuring company culture, also assess sub-cultures, i.e., the cultures in particular business units, departments and smaller parts of the company. (See Petry, "Assessing Corporate Culture," *ethikos* 18 no. 5 (Mar./Apr. 2005): 1, 3.)

306 **Outside SME reviews.** Have an outside firm with specific risk-area compliance and ethics expertise conduct an independent review and assessment of specific risk area compliance programs, such as those in the environmental, antitrust or FCPA areas.

307   **Assigned follow-ups.** For each review, assessment or other measurement step, assign a specific manager responsibility to follow up on all of the findings and recommendations, so that the loop is always closed.

308   **Program dashboards.** Have a system for monitoring key performance indicators on a real time basis, such as patterns in helpline calls, patterns in disciplinary cases, and training attendance in specific work units. (See Singer, "Boeing Company's Ethics Improvements Take Flight," *ethikos* 20 no. 1 (July/Aug. 2006): 5, 6.)

309   **Key performance indicators.** Establish key performance indicators for the program and assign rating numbers to each element and sub-element. (See Sharpe, "Checking Your Compliance Program's Performance—By the Numbers," *ethikos* 16 no. 5 (May/June 2003): 10.)

310   **Statistical analysis.** In some compliance areas it may be possible to run statistical analyses to kick out red flags. For example, the government reportedly does this to flush out market allocation and other collusive bidding schemes.

L. USSGs item 6, discipline

Companies have to show that they are serious about their compliance and ethics programs through the use of discipline. The items here cover part of item 6 in the USSGs.

311 **Disciplinary guides.** Have a set of disciplinary guides for compliance/ethics cases. These can include aggravating and mitigating factors. (See Murphy, "Taking a Disciplined Approach to Discipline: Enforcing Compliance Standards," *ethikos* 13 no. 5 (Mar./Apr. 2000): 4; HHS, "OIG Compliance Program Guidance for Pharmaceutical Manufacturers," *Federal Register* 68 (May 5, 2003): 23,731, 23,741-42.)

312 **Tough at the top.** Provide in the disciplinary guides an indication that the standards and sanctions are tougher the higher up one is in the corporate hierarchy. This step helps address the concern of employees and the government that the company will resort to scapegoating junior level employees to protect those at the top.

313 **Failure to take steps.** Include "failure to take reasonable steps to prevent and detect misconduct" as a disciplinary factor in the disciplinary guidelines and/or the code of conduct. (See HHS, "OIG Compliance Program Guidance for Pharmaceutical Manufacturers," *Federal Register* 68 (May 5, 2003): 23,731, 23,742; Murphy, "Taking a Disciplined Approach to Discipline: Enforcing Compliance Standards," *ethikos* 13 no. 5 (Mar./Apr. 2000): 4-5, 8.)

314 **Disciplinary review panel.** Have one review panel to help assure consistency in compliance and ethics disciplinary cases throughout the company. (See "In Search of Disciplinary Consistency," *ethikos* 14 no. 4 (Jan./Feb. 2001): 12-13.)

315 **Probation.** Use a form of probation for light disciplinary cases. Those subject to probation would report regularly to a lawyer or compliance and ethics professional for guidance on their rehabilitation. (See Murphy, "Taking a Disciplined Approach to Discipline: Enforcing Compliance Standards," *ethikos* 13 no. 5 (Mar./Apr. 2000): 4, 6.)

316 **Ineligibility for promotion.** One form of discipline is to place a violator on a list of those who are ineligible for promotion, at least for a period of probation after a violation. (See Murphy, "Taking a Disciplined Approach to Discipline: Enforcing Compliance Standards," *ethikos* 13 no. 5 (Mar./Apr. 2000): 4, 6.)

317 **Senior manager disciplinary cases.** Review with the board any disciplinary cases involving senior managers, including any decision not to investigate or impose discipline on a senior person. (See Murphy, "Taking a Disciplined Approach to Discipline: Enforcing Compliance Standards," *ethikos* 13 no. 5 (Mar./Apr. 2000): 4, 8.)

318 **C&E input.** Require input or approval from the compliance and ethics office for compliance-related disciplinary cases. (See Murphy, "Taking a Disciplined Approach to Discipline: Enforcing Compliance Standards," *ethikos* 13 no. 5 (Mar./Apr. 2000): 4, 5.)

319 **Disciplinary database.** Maintain a database of disciplinary cases to help ensure consistency. (See "In Search of Disciplinary Consistency," *ethikos* 14 no. 4 (Jan./Feb. 2001): 12, 13.)

320 **Escalation requirement.** Any time the compliance and ethics professionals' disciplinary recommendation is not followed, require that this be escalated to the board. (See *SEC v. Prudential Securities, Inc.*, CV93-2164 (D.D.C., Oct. 21, 1993); Jordan & Murphy, "Compliance Programs: What the Government Really Wants," *ACCA Docket* (July/Aug. 1996): 10.)

321 **Setting a range.** Establish a range of disciplinary options for various types of offenses, based on the compliance and ethics office's past experiences. (See Singer, "How Dow Chemical Centralized its Investigations Process," *ethikos* 19 no. 1 (July/Aug. 2005): 1, 4; Murphy, "Taking a Disciplined Approach to Discipline: Enforcing Compliance Standards," *ethikos* 13 no. 5 (Mar./Apr. 2000): 4, 6.)

322 **Fairness in disciplinary process.** Set standards in advance to ensure fairness in the disciplinary process and to avoid ambiguity and ad hoc decisions on such questions as confronting witnesses and notice of allegations. (See Murphy, "Taking a Disciplined Approach to Discipline: Enforcing Compliance Standards," *ethikos* 13 no. 5 (Mar./Apr. 2000): 4, 7.)

323 **Appeals.** Determine in advance whether there should be any appeals process for disciplinary decisions, to avoid any appearance of favoritism if higher level officials face discipline and go over the heads of the decision makers. (See Murphy, "Taking a Disciplined Approach to Discipline: Enforcing Compliance Standards," *ethikos* 13 no. 5 (Mar./Apr. 2000): 4, 7.)

324 **Legal guidance.** Have a company labor lawyer assigned to assist in all compliance disciplinary cases. (See Murphy, "Taking a Disciplined Approach to Discipline: Enforcing Compliance Standards," *ethikos* 13 no. 5 (Mar./Apr. 2000): 4, 8.)

M. USSGs item 6, incentives, rewards, recognition

Punishment is only half the picture; compliance and ethics programs also have to use incentives to be effective. Here are ways to meet this part of the USSGs item 6 standard.

325 **Training requirements.** Tie the completion of all applicable compliance and ethics training to an employee's ability to obtain a satisfactory annual assessment, be eligible for promotion, or receive a raise. (See Roach & Davis, "Establishing a Culture of Ethics and Integrity in Government," *ethikos* 21 no. 2 (Sept./Oct. 2007): 1, 4; Sigler & Murphy, *Interactive Corporate Compliance: An Alternative to Regulatory Compulsion* (Westport, CT: Quorum Books, 1988): 86, 90.)

326 **Bonus eligibility.** Develop specific, objectively measurable ethics and compliance objectives. Measure senior business leaders on their business units' fulfillment of those objectives. Their ratings in these categories can then act as a threshold for determining bonus eligibility. (See *Building Incentives in Your Compliance & Ethics Program* (Minneapolis: Society of Corporate Compliance and Ethics, 2007), http://www.corporatecompliance.org/Content/NavigationMenu/Resources/Issues Answers/DRAFTwhitepaper-BuildingIncentivesCompliance_WOappdx.pdf.; Dan Roach).

327 **Senior managers' incentive comp.** Tie a percentage of senior managers' incentive and bonus compensation to their compliance and ethics performance. (See Singer, "A Computer Software Giant Takes Time Out for Compliance," *ethikos* 21 no. 2 (Sept./Oct. 2007): 5, 7; Sigler & Murphy, *Interactive Corporate Compliance: An Alternative to Regulatory Compulsion* (Westport, CT: Quorum Books, 1988): 83; Singer, "At Tenet Healthcare: Linking Ethics to Compensation," *ethikos* 14 no. 4 (Jan./Feb. 2001): 4.)

328 **Succession planning.** If the company does succession planning or identifies high potential employees for future leadership positions, have compliance and ethics commitment and performance as an important element in that process. (See *Building Incentives in Your Compliance & Ethics Program* (Minneapolis: Society of Corporate Compliance and Ethics, 2007), http://www.corporatecompliance.org/Content/NavigationMenu/Resources/IssuesAnswers/DRAFTwhitepaper-BuildingIncentivesCompliance_WOappdx.pdf.)

329 **Departmental performance.** Evaluate entire departments' performance based on how well they followed the company's compliance and ethics standards. (See Murphy, "Compliance Guidance From the United Kingdom," *ethikos* 20 no. 5 (Mar./Apr. 2007): 5, 6.)

330 **Company rewards programs.** Add compliance and ethics-related factors into the criteria for company rewards and recognition programs. (See *Building Incentives in Your Compliance & Ethics Program* (Minneapolis: Society of Corporate Compliance and Ethics, 2007), http://www.corporatecompliance.org/Content/NavigationMenu/Resources/IssuesAnswers/DRAFTwhitepaper-BuildingIncentivesCompliance_WOappdx.pdf.)

331 **Recognition letters.** One of the easiest and least expensive forms of reward for contributions to the compliance and ethics program is the recognition letter from a senior executive, such as the CEO or the compliance officer. (See Murphy & Vigale, "The Role of Incentives in Compliance Programs," *ethikos* 18 no. 6 (May/June 2005): 8, 10-11; Singer, "At Tenet Healthcare: Linking Ethics to Compensation," *ethikos* 14 no. 4 (Jan./Feb. 2001): 4-5; *Building Incentives in Your Compliance & Ethics Program* (Minneapolis: Society of Corporate Compliance and Ethics, 2007), http://www.corporatecompliance.org/Content/NavigationMenu/Resources/IssuesAnswers/DRAFTwhitepaper-BuildingIncentivesCompliance_WOappdx.pdf.)

332 **"Ethics film festival."** Stage an "ethics film festival," and have a contest for employees to produce their own, short compliance and ethics video; then have a recognition ceremony for the best ones. (See Sears, "Lights! Camera! Action! Lockheed Martin's Ethics Film Festival," *ethikos* 17 no. 4 (Jan/Feb 2004): 8.)

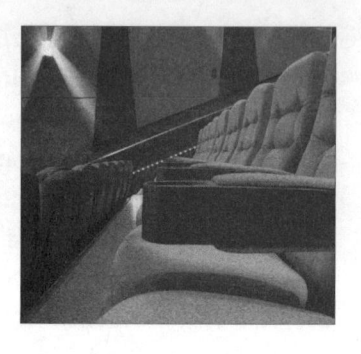

333 **1001 rewards.** For ideas on how to reward employees, which could be used to recognize strong compliance and ethics performance, see Nelson, *1001 Ways to Reward Employees* (New York: Workman Publishing Co.; 1994).)

334 **Rewards for work groups.** Provide rewards to recognize entire work groups. For example, the company could offer a free lunch to the work group that completes the code training first. (See *Building Incentives in Your Compliance & Ethics Program* (Minneapolis: Society of Corporate Compliance and Ethics, 2007), http://www.corporatecompliance.org/Content/NavigationMenu/Resources/IssuesAnswers/DRAFTwhitepaper-Building-IncentivesCompliance_WOappdx.pdf; Webb, "Ottenberg's: A Recipe for Rewarding Safety: Bakery's Incentive Program Cuts Costs, Improves Productivity," *Washington Post* (Feb. 19, 1990): F11.)

335 **Recognizing C&E staff.** Have a program for recognizing the achievements of the compliance and ethics staff, singling out the top performers for special recognition. (See *Building Incentives in Your Compliance & Ethics Program* (Minneapolis: Society of Corporate Compliance and Ethics, 2007), http://www.corporatecompliance.org/Content/NavigationMenu/Resources/IssuesAnswers/DRAFTwhitepaper-BuildingIncentivesCompliance_WOappdx.pdf.)

336 **Insulate C&E staff's rewards.** Provide that the compliance and ethics staff's bonus and reward treatment is not to be tied to the functions they are responsible for overseeing. For example, those monitoring sales conduct would not have their bonuses tied to sales objectives. (See Jordan & Murphy, "Compliance Programs: What the Government Really Wants," *ACCA Docket* (July/Aug. 1996): 10, 22; *United States v. C.R. Bard Inc.*, CV93-10276-T, plea agreement (D. Mass; Oct. 14, 1993); Sigler & Murphy, *Interactive Corporate Compliance: An Alternative to Regulatory Compulsion* (Westport, CT: Quorum Books, 1988): 83.)

337 **Integrity evaluation form.** Use an integrity evaluation form as part of managers' annual evaluations, including such elements as the manager's use of the code of conduct, attendance at compliance training, and support of subordinates who raise compliance issues. (See Murphy & Vigale, "The Role of Incentives in Compliance Programs," *ethikos* 18 no. 5 (May/June 2005): 8, 10-11.)

338 **Personal development plans.** For those whose compliance and ethics evaluations yield poor results, require personal development plans to monitor and improve their performance. (See Bell, "How Memorial Health measures the ethics performance of its senior managers," *ethikos* 18 no. 4(Jan./Feb. 2005): 8, 10.)

339 **360 degree reviews.** For input on managers' compliance and ethics assessments, conduct 360 reviews of each manager's peers, subordinates and supervisors. (See Singer, "Fannie Mae Rates Managers on Integrity and Honesty," *ethikos* 17 no. 1 (July/Aug. 2003): 4.)

340 **Fostering ethical behavior.** Have supervisors and managers evaluated on their efforts to promote ethical and compliant behavior. (See Jordan & Murphy, "Compliance Programs: What the Government Really Wants," *ACCA Docket* (July/Aug. 1996): 10, 22; HHS, "OIG Compliance Program Guidance for Pharmaceutical Manufacturers," *Federal Register* 68 (May 5, 2003): 23,731, 23,732-733.)

341 **Spot awards.** Give employees immediate, on the spot, tangible rewards for doing something positive, like offering a solution to a problem that meets business needs but also enhances ethics and compliance. (See Singer, "TAP Pharma Isn't Afraid to Show 'a Little Levity,'" *ethikos* 19 no. 5 (Mar./Apr. 2006): 16, 18.)

342 **Input into incentive/reward plans.** Require all incentive, evaluation and reward plans and programs to be reviewed first by compliance and ethics professionals, to avoid motivating improper behavior. (See Murphy & Vigale, "The Role of Incentives in Compliance Programs," *ethikos* 18 no. 6 (May/June 2005): 8, 11.)

N. USSGs item 7, responses and investigations

When a compliance or ethics problem is found, companies have to respond, as established under item 7 of the USSGs. Here are ideas for meeting this standard.

343 **Investigation standards.** Have standards for investigations; these could be set out in an investigations manual. This step would help assure that all investigations company-wide meet certain standards of conduct.

344 **Train investigators.** Have training for investigators on the investigation standards and how to investigate effectively. Have coverage on how to conduct interviews, including conducting practice interviews. (See Bavuso & Murphy, "The Compliance Investigation: How to Conduct Effective Interviews," *Prevention of Corporate Liability Current Report* 11 (July 21, 2003): 72; Singer, "How Dow Chemical Centralized its Investigations Process," *ethikos* 19 no. 1 (July/Aug. 2005): 1, 4.)

345 **Centralize and coordinate.** Have a company-wide system for coordinating and monitoring all compliance-related investigations, not just those arising from the helpline or managed by the compliance and ethics group. These might include HR, audit, security, legal, etc. This centralized approach helps ensure one consistent report to management and the board. (See Singer, "How Dow Chemical Centralized its Investigations Process," *ethikos* 19 no. 1 (July/Aug. 2005): 1.)

346 **Forensic auditors.** Have an auditor trained in forensic accounting to assist in internal investigations; this person could also become a certified fraud examiner.

347 **Root cause analysis.** Require in the investigations manual or some other policy covering investigations, that every investigation include a root cause analysis to determine the causes of violations, consistent with the requirements of USSGs item 7.

348 **Benchmark response times.** Consider setting benchmark response target times for different categories of investigations. An estimate of the usual time for investigating particular types of matters would be set; investigations exceeding that time would be placed on an exceptions report for tracking purposes. This avoids unrealistic deadlines, but helps monitor progress.

349 **Voluntary disclosure policy.** Have a standard/policy regarding voluntary disclosure of violations to appropriate governmental authorities. This could be included in the board's resolution implementing the compliance and ethics program.

350 **Confidentiality notice.** Consider giving a written notice to all those to be interviewed in an internal investigation, stating the need for confidentiality and non-retaliation, commitment to the code of conduct, and other matters related to the investigation.

351 **Post-mortems.** Stage a post-mortem session with work groups that have experienced an investigation, to provide closure and air concerns. (See "Investigation, Termination—and the Aftermath," *ethikos* 11 no. 4 (Jan./Feb. 1998): 5.)

352   **Closure letters.** Provide closure letters to those interviewed in an investigation, letting them know that the investigation has been concluded, and reminding them of important points such as the rule against retaliation. Otherwise, if an investigation has been kept confidential, employees may remain worried about what they may have said in an interview and whether they did something wrong. (See "Investigation, Termination—and the Aftermath," *ethikos* 11 no. 4 (Jan./Feb. 1998): 5.)

353   **Investigation FAQs.** Create FAQs for those participating in or affected by investigations, covering questions like "Why are you interviewing me?" and "Do I have to answer your questions?" Taking this step helps employees understand what is going on in investigations.

354   **Cell phones.** At the start of an interview make it clear that the interviewee is not to be interrupted by cell phone, pager or Blackberry. The interviewers may set an example by taking out their phones and turning them off. (See Bavuso & Murphy, "The Compliance Investigation: How to Conduct Effective Interviews," *Prevention of Corporate Liability Current Report* 11 (July 21, 2003): 70, 72.)

355   **Two interviewers.** Use two interviewers in investigation interviews, so there is always a witness, and one person can concentrate on taking notes. (See Bavuso & Murphy, "The Compliance Investigation: How to Conduct Effective Interviews," *Prevention of Corporate Liability Current Report* 11 (July 21, 2003): 72.)

356   **Chronology.** When conducting investigations, create a timeline or chronology that is expanded and annotated as the investigation progresses. (See Bavuso & Murphy, "The Compliance Investigation: How to Conduct Effective Interviews," *Prevention of Corporate Liability Current Report* 11 (July 21, 2003): 70, 72.)

357 **Silence in interviews.** Use silence as a questioning technique. If the interviewers remain silent after the interviewee answers a question, the interviewee may well volunteer more information to fill the void. (See Bavuso & Murphy, "The Compliance Investigation: How to Conduct Effective Interviews," *Prevention of Corporate Liability Current Report* 11 (July 21, 2003): 70, 72.)

358 **Repeated questions.** In investigation interviews, return to certain important questions more than once, since people tend to remember things in waves. When the question is asked again (with slight variations) the interviewee may well remember more details. (See Bavuso & Murphy, "The Compliance Investigation: How to Conduct Effective Interviews," *Prevention of Corporate Liability Current Report* 11 (July 21, 2003): 70, 72.)

359 **Establish a range.** When asking factual, descriptive questions, if an interviewee cannot give a specific description, ask questions that help establish a range. For example, if the interviewee cannot remember the number of people present at an event, ask if it was more or less than 20. This helps clarify the information, and may help restore the interviewee's memory. (See Bavuso & Murphy, "The Compliance Investigation: How to Conduct Effective Interviews," *Prevention of Corporate Liability Current Report* 11 (July 21, 2003): 70, 72.)

360 **Summarize for interviewees.** During interviews, occasionally summarize what the interviewee has said. This helps confirm the accuracy of the information, and may stimulate the interviewee to provide additional information. (See Bavuso & Murphy, "The Compliance Investigation: How to Conduct Effective Interviews," *Prevention of Corporate Liability Current Report* 11 (July 21, 2003): 71, 72.)

361　**Open-ended last question.** At the end of an investigation interview, ask an open-ended question, such as, "Is there anything I should have asked but didn't?" or "Is there anything else I should know?" At the end of the interview, the interviewee may then be thinking about a difficult point that was not covered, and this question may trigger release of that sensitive information. (See Bavuso & Murphy, "The Compliance Investigation: How to Conduct Effective Interviews," *Prevention of Corporate Liability Current Report* 11 (July 21, 2003): 71, 72.)

362　**"Upjohn" letter.** If a lawyer is conducting the investigation interviews, have an "Upjohn" letter, explaining that counsel represents the company, not the interviewee. (See Murphy, "Surviving the Antitrust Compliance Audit," *Antitrust Law Journal* 59 (1991): 953, 960-61.)

363　**Case management system.** Have an electronic case management system to keep track of all compliance and ethics investigations, and determine trends. (See Muse, "Hotlines Must Adapt to an Ever-Changing Global Environment," *ethikos* 20 no. 4 (Jan./Feb. 2007): 11, 12.)

364　**Understanding privileges.** For those conducting investigations, provide training and a guide on privileges and confidentiality so it is known when and how to invoke privilege. Even lawyers sometimes forget that there are more privilege protections than just attorney-client. (See Kaplan & Murphy, *Compliance Programs and the Corporate Sentencing Guidelines* (Eagan, MN: Thomson/West; 1993 & Ann'l Supp): Sections 5:38-5:48.)

365　**Opportunities to improve.** Train investigators to treat every investigation as an opportunity to improve the compliance program. Even when allegations are not substantiated, the interviews and document reviews may reveal weaknesses in the compliance program and related control systems. Investigators could be conditioned to seek out these problems and report on them.

366 **Not just bad news.** Include positive findings in the investigation report. In addition to determining what went wrong, point out things that were done right, such as employee awareness of training, willingness to call the helpline, etc. (See Murphy, "Surviving the Antitrust Compliance Audit," *Antitrust Law Journal* 59 (1991): 953, 963.)

367 **Find it/fix it.** Have the final investigation report reflect not only that you found problems, but that you fixed them. Include a description in the final written report of what was done to fix the problems. (See Murphy, "Surviving the Antitrust Compliance Audit," *Antitrust Law Journal* 59 (1991): 953, 963.)

368 **Protecting final reports.** Consider the full range of privilege and confidentiality protections for the investigation report. Take these into account in marking the report, and in drafting the report's introduction. (See Murphy, "Surviving the Antitrust Compliance Audit," *Antitrust Law Journal* 59 (1991): 953, 964.)

O. USSGs item c, risk assessment

Companies need to determine what compliance and ethics risks they face. This list covers the risk assessment element of USSGs item c.

369 **Compliance committee agenda.** Include risk assessment as a regular agenda item in compliance committee meetings. This helps keep the assessment process ongoing.

370 **Risk SME presentations.** Have each risk area subject matter expert address the compliance committee from time to time on developments in his/her risk area.

371 **Risk list.** Start with a list of risks applicable to most companies. While no off-the-shelf list is adequate, starting with a standard risk helps avoid missing risks that might otherwise be overlooked. (See "App. 6-A: Compliance Program Inventory," in Kaplan & Murphy, *Compliance Programs and the Corporate Sentencing Guidelines* (Eagan, MN: Thomson/West; 1993 & Ann'l Supp).)

372 **Risk assessment grid.** Plot and assess risks on a grid, using the types of risks (e.g., antitrust, harassment, environmental, etc.) on the vertical plane. On the horizontal plane, have factors relating to probability of occurrence and seriousness of impact.

373 **3-D matrix.** Analyze risk on a three-dimensional matrix, covering types of risk, units of the business, and compliance program steps. (See Kaplan, "Thinking Inside the Box: Risk Analysis in Three Dimensions," *ethikos* 14 no. 2 (Sept./Oct. 2000): 1; Kaplan, "Compliance Risk Analyses: Reasons and Capacities for Wrongdoing," *ethikos* 16 no. 4 (Jan./Feb. 2003): 5.)

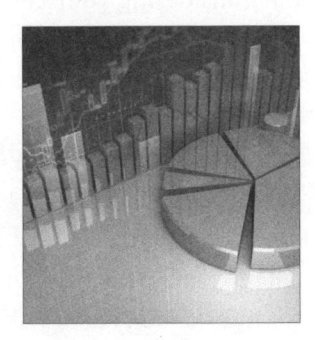

374 **Capacities and motives.** When conducting risk assessments, analyze who and what positions have the ability to commit violations, and determine what the motivations might be. (See Kaplan, "Compliance Risk Analyses: Reasons and Capacities for Wrongdoing," *ethikos* 16 no. 4 (Jan./Feb. 2003): 5.)

375 **Risk enhancers.** Risk analysis can consider elements that increase the likelihood of certain violations, such as remoteness from headquarters and access to advanced technology. (See Kaplan, "Compliance Risk Analyses: Reasons and Capacities for Wrongdoing," *ethikos* 16 no. 4 (Jan./Feb. 2003): 5, 7.)

376 **Clarification questions.** When conducting risk assessments, ask these five questions to clarify the risks: what does the company make/provide, who is involved, who buys it, how do you get business and how does payment occur. (See Kaplan, "Five Questions for a Risk Analysis," *ethikos* 14 no. 6 (May/June 2001): 4.)

377 **Prioritize risks.** Use a system to prioritize risks, such as numbers or colors to indicate which risks are most important and require increased attention. (See Kaplan, "The Ethics Officer Association's Risk Assessment Survey," *ethikos* 18 no. 3 (Nov./Dec. 2004): 1, 3.)

378 **Risk mitigation factors.** Assess the likelihood of the risks in two ways: first, without considering your control and compliance efforts, and then taking risk mitigation factors into account.

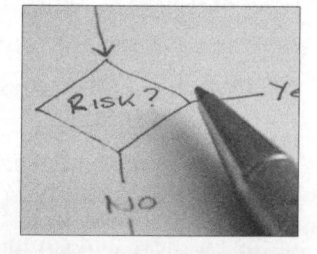

379 **Others' codes.** Review other companies' codes of conduct, usually available on the Internet, to determine what risks they are including.

380 **Industry trade publications.** Review industry trade publications for information about risks affecting the industry that might also apply to the company. (See Kaplan, "The Ethics Officer Association's Risk Assessment Survey," *ethikos* 18 no. 3 (Nov./Dec. 2004): 1, 3.)

381 **Survey of managers.** Survey managers throughout the business on their assessment of the compliance and ethics risks; questionnaires and interviews can be used for this purpose. (See Singer, "Needed from Bertelsmann's Ethics & Compliance Officer: A 'Diplomatic Effort,'" *ethikos* 17 no. 2 (Sept./Oct. 2003): 7-8.)

382 **Focus groups.** Use focus groups to discuss and surface information about company risks. (See Kaplan, "The Ethics Officer Association's Risk Assessment Survey," *ethikos* 18 no. 3 (Nov./Dec. 2004): 1, 3.)

383 **Interview outside counsel and consultants.** In addition to surveying and interviewing insiders, also talk with those outside who are familiar with the company and its risks, such as outside counsel and consultants. (See Kaplan, "The Ethics Officer Association's Risk Assessment Survey," *ethikos* 18 no. 3 (Nov./Dec. 2004): 1, 3.)

384 **Industry practices groups.** Discuss the developing and potential industry compliance risks at industry practices groups. (See Murphy, "Industry Practices Groups: Why and How," *ethikos* 20 no. 1 (July/Aug 2006): 12, 13-14.)

385 **Industry practices groups' outside speakers.** At industry practices group meetings, invite experienced outside counsel and government representatives to give their views on emerging risks. If the group includes major companies, many outside counsel will do this for free as a marketing opportunity.

386 **Trade associations.** Trade associations can provide a forum for discussing and exchanging information on compliance risks in your industry. (See Kaplan, "Compliance Programs for Smaller Companies," *ethikos* 21 no. 4 (Jan./Feb. 2008): 6, 7-8.)

387 **Wall Street Journal.** Monitor the *Wall Street Journal* regularly for current news of emerging compliance risk developments.

388 **Monitor enforcement priorities.** Have a process for monitoring what various government enforcement agencies are saying about their enforcement priorities. For example, in health care in the U.S., the office of Inspector General in Health and Human Services (HHS) provides guidance on its enforcement focus; other agencies may indicate their priorities in a less formal but still public way.

389 **Third-party risks.** Consider the risks posed by third parties you do business with, e.g., customers, suppliers, partners, etc., as an element of the risk assessment.

390 **Board risk assessment.** Have a separate assessment of what compliance and ethics risks apply particularly to the board. (See Kaplan, "The Tone at the Middle," *ethikos* 20 no. 2 (Sept./Oct. 2006): 5, 6.)

391 **SME councils.** Have a committee or council made up of those responsible for the compliance efforts in the different compliance risk areas. This committee could meet periodically with the chief compliance and ethics officer to assess compliance risks in the different subject areas. (See Scarpino, "NCR Corporation's Fourfold Ethics & Compliance Model," *ethikos* 20 no. 1 (July/Aug. 2006): 7, 9, 17.)

392 **Use of counsel.** Companies may have risk assessment work done under the direction and control of legal counsel to assert attorney-client privilege. (See Kaplan, "The Ethics Officer Association's Risk Assessment Survey," *ethikos* 18 no. 3 (Nov./Dec. 2004): 1, 3.)

393 **RAMP.** Require a risk assessment and management plan ("RAMP") for all proposed acquisitions and new business ventures, to ensure that compliance risks are assessed, and that there is a plan for managing them as the new business proceeds. (See Murphy, "Reducing Foreign Corrupt Practices Act Risk: An Effective Self-Policing Program," *Corporate Conduct Quarterly* (now *ethikos*) 5 (1996): 28, 37.)

P. Industry practices, benchmarking

Companies need to know how their compliance and ethics programs stack up against others', so they can meet the industry practices standard of the USSGs commentary. Companies can use these ideas to help ensure they are keeping up with industry practices.

394 **Local best practices forums.** Form a local, cross-industry best practices compliance/ethics forum to exchange program ideas. (See Lipps, "Regional Business Ethics Roundtables: The Greater Houston Experience," *ethikos* 21 no.2 (Sept./Oct. 2007): 11; Murphy, "Industry Practices Groups: Why and How," *ethikos* 20 no. 1 (July/Aug 2006): 12, 13.)

395 **Universities.** Ask a local university to serve as host for the local industry practices forum.

396 **Industry practice groups.** Form an industry practices group in your industry, but include antitrust counsel to minimize risks. (See Murphy, "Industry Practices Groups: Why and How," *ethikos* 20 no. 1 (July/Aug 2006): 12.)

397 **Roundtable discussions.** Use roundtable discussions at compliance practices forums, where each company discusses its experiences and issues, with input from all participating companies. (See Murphy, "Industry Practices Groups: Why and How," *ethikos* 20 no. 1 (July/Aug 2006): 12, 15.)

398 **Industry forum coordinators.** Recruit a law firm to take on the role of compliance practices group coordinator. The firm may do this as a matter of client development. (See Murphy, "Industry Practices Groups: Why and How," *ethikos* 20 no. 1 (July/Aug 2006): 12, 14.)

399 **Vendor demonstrations.** At compliance practices forums, invite competing vendors in to make presentations, so the members (acting individually and not as a group) can get a quick overview of industry practices and vendor offerings in the area being covered. (See Murphy, "Industry Practices Groups: Why and How," *ethikos* 20 no. 1 (July/Aug 2006): 12, 15.)

400 **Compliance forum sub-groups.** In a compliance forum it may be useful to develop sub-groups to focus on specific issues, like global programs (for groups where some are domestic only and others are global), environmental risks, etc. (See Murphy, "Industry Practices Groups: Why and How," *ethikos* 20 no. 1 (July/Aug 2006): 12, 16.)

401 **Guides for forming forums.** Provide guides to your company's compliance managers around the world on how to form local compliance practices forums with their peers at other companies in that region.

402 **Government speakers.** Invite government officials to speak occasionally at your compliance practices group's sessions. This tactic shows you are open to outside ideas, and visibly demonstrates to those in government that your industry takes seriously its commitment to compliance and ethics. (See Murphy, "Industry Practices Groups: Why and How," *ethikos* 20 no. 1 (July/Aug 2006): 12, 15.)

403 **Compliance libraries.** Visit and review libraries of compliance and ethics materials for benchmarking and comparison. Such libraries are maintained by the Defense Industry Initiative for its members, and by SCCE for its members, see http://www.corporatecompliance.org/Content/NavigationMenu/Resources/JEMurphyLibrary/default.htm.)

404 *ethikos.* Subscribe to *ethikos* and review back issues for practical ideas for your compliance program, and information on what other companies are doing. (See http://www.ethikosjournal.com/.)

405 **Trade associations.** In some environments, trade associations may provide guidelines for compliance programs in their industry. (See Bevilacqua, "Corporate Compliance Programs Under Italian Law," *ethikos* 20 no. 3 (Nov./Dec.2006): 1, 4.)

406 **SCCE.** Join the Society of Corporate Compliance and Ethics and use its Web site and opportunities for networking to obtain information on best practices and industry practice. (See www.corporatecompliance.org.)

SOCIETY OF CORPORATE
COMPLIANCE AND ETHICS

Q. Third parties, joint ventures

Not just employees, but agents, consultants and other third parties can affect a company's compliance and ethics risk profile. Agents are also referenced in the USSGs. Here are ideas for covering third parties.

407 **Vendor workshops.** Hold a workshop for vendors, suppliers and other business partners to help them develop their own compliance and ethics programs.

408 **Train the purchasing department.** Provide training to the company's purchasing department so they can understand and support the company's approach to compliance regarding third parties and can help promote compliance and ethics among suppliers. (See Pompa & Petry, "More Companies Are Looking at Ethics in the 'Extended Organization,'" *ethikos* 12 no. 5 (Mar./Apr. 1999): 7, 8.)

409 **Third party compliance manual.** Develop a compliance manual for suppliers and other third parties that do business with the company. This document addresses their conduct when acting for the company.

410 **Availability of helpline.** Make your reporting and helpline system available to agents and other third parties. You can include the helpline number in vendor remittances. (See Martens & Crowell, "Whistleblowing: A Global Perspective (Part II)," *ethikos* 16 no. 1 (July/Aug. 2002): 9, 10.; Doug Beeuwsaert.)

411 **Due diligence checklist.** Have a due diligence checklist regarding compliance and ethics for selection of third parties, to include items such as determining whether the third party has a program with all the Sentencing Guidelines elements.

412 **Due diligence folder.** Require a due diligence folder on each agent/third party, or at least those performing the highest risk functions. (See Murphy, "Reducing Foreign Corrupt Practices Act Risk: An Effective Self-Policing Program," *Corporate Conduct Quarterly* (now *ethikos*) 5 (1996): 28, 37.)

413 **Limit who can retain agents.** Place limits on who may retain third parties (especially high-risk ones such as foreign agents and environmental contractors), and require compliance and ethics training for all those with such retention authority.

414 **Contractual standards.** Include in contracts with agents, suppliers and other third parties provisions relating to that third party's conduct on behalf of the company. Areas covered can include improper gifts, bribery, export control, privacy, and any other risk areas related to work done for the company. (See Boehme & Murphy, "No Place to Hide: Early Lessons From the Siemens Case," *ethikos* 21 no. 3 (Nov./Dec. 2007): 10, 11.)

415 **Third-party discipline.** Provide by contract that your company may require contractors and agents to remove specific employees from any matters related to the company if those employees violate the company's compliance and ethics standards. (See Murphy, "Taking a Disciplined Approach to Discipline: Enforcing Compliance Standards," *ethikos* 13 no. 5 (Mar./Apr. 2000): 4, 11.)

416 **Reps and warranties.** Require compliance-related reps and warranties from contractors and agents. These can include commitments to compliance and representations about the third party's prior conduct. (See Murphy, "Reducing Foreign Corrupt Practices Act Risk: An Effective Self-Policing Program," *Corporate Conduct Quarterly* (now *ethikos*) 5 (1996): 28, 30.)

417 **Third-party compliance programs.** Include in contracts with agents, suppliers and other third parties some provisions requiring third parties have a compliance and ethics program based on the Sentencing Guidelines standards. (See Walker, "Extending Compliance Requirements to Suppliers and Other Third Parties," *ethikos* 19 no. 6 (May/June 2006): 5, 7, 8.)

418 **JV compliance programs.** Have a company policy that requires all joint ventures in which the company has a controlling interest to have compliance programs, and require the company to use its best efforts to establish one in ventures in which it has only a minority interest. Include this requirement for establishing a compliance and ethics program in the standard terms for any joint venture.

419 **JV controlling interests.** For joint ventures where the company has a controlling interest, provide that the company's compliance officer has at least some supervisory authority over the venture's compliance officer.

420 **Vendor letters.** Use "vendor letters" to third parties, stating your gifts and conflicts policies, covering other elements of your code that may apply to dealings with third parties, and including your helpline number. (See Singer, "Developing *Effective* Helplines: Shell Oil and Lubrizol," *ethikos* 19 no. 2 (Sept./Oct. 2005): 5, 7.)

421 **Duty to report.** Include in contracts with third parties a duty to report to the company any instances or allegations of illegal or unethical conduct involving work for your company.

422 **Disclosure to the government.** Non-disclosure agreements with third parties can have an exception giving the company the authority to disclose wrongdoing to government agencies.

423 **Cooperation in investigations.** Include in contracts with third parties a requirement to cooperate in company compliance and ethics investigations. (See Kaplan, Murphy & Swenson, "Are Conflicts of Interest Your Program's Achilles Heel?" *ethikos* 15 no. 2 (Sept./Oct. 2001): 1, 16.)

424 **Auditing third parties.** A company may provide by contract the right to audit its agents' conduct, including a review of their books and records and their operations. (See Walker, "Extending Compliance Requirements to Suppliers and Other Third Parties," *ethikos* 19 no. 6 (May/June 2006): 5, 6; Sigler & Murphy, *Interactive Corporate Compliance: An Alternative to Regulatory Compulsion* (Westport, CT: Quorum Books, 1988): 90-91.)

425 **Code to third parties.** Provide the company's code of conduct to non-employees, such as temporary employees, contract employees and consultants. (See Petry, "EOA Survey: Companies Seeking to Integrate Ethics Through the Whole Organization," *ethikos* 15 no. 1 (July/Aug. 2001): 1, 3.)

R. Miscellaneous/other

Not all compliance elements fit neatly within the USSGs structure. Here are some additional ideas to consider.

426 **Prepare and save presentations.** Prepare a presentation on the program for the government or other skeptical third party. Keep this ready in a binder, and update it with each change in your program. But keep older, dated records also, since any presentation may need to address program conditions for a specific time period preceding an alleged violation.

427 **Practice presentation.** Do a practice presentation of your program to someone acting as a government official, judge, jury, or other skeptical third party. Use the feedback to update the presentation and fix weaknesses in the underlying program.

428 **Target company's program.** Include a review of a target company's compliance and ethics program in the scope of acquisition due diligence. (See Jordan & Murphy, "Are You Buying Trouble? Ignoring Target Company's Compliance Efforts Could Be Folly," *Prevention of Corporate Liability Current Report* 5 (Oct. 20, 1997): 12.)

429 **Contingency plan.** Have a contingency plan for compliance emergencies, including how to explain to the press the role of the compliance and ethics program. The plan would include a team of key players and information on how to contact them 24 hours per day. (See Murphy, "How to Respond to Compliance Failures," *ALI-ABA Course Materials Journal* 16 (June 1992): 7.)

430 **Contingency plan try-out.** Have a dry run of the compliance emergency contingency plan to test it out and discover any gaps, before an actual emergency occurs.

431 **SCCE bibliography.** Use the bibliography on the SCCE members' Web site for sources of ideas and guidance on your compliance program.

432 **Compliance program standards.** Use the international section of the SCCE Web site for information about various nations' and stock exchanges' requirements and standards for compliance programs. (See http://www.corporatecompliance.org/AM/Template.cfm?Section=International.)

433 **Securities lawyers' escalation.** Have a formal, written policy requiring lawyers to escalate compliance issues, following the provisions of Sarbanes Oxley and SEC rules regarding securities lawyers.

434 **All lawyers' escalation.** Expand the lawyers' escalation policy beyond the requirements of the SEC's rules, to extend to all lawyers (not just securities lawyers) on all compliance issues (not just securities law issues), so that lawyers would escalate these issues to senior management and the board.

435 **Lawyers' training.** Provide training for lawyers regarding the lawyers' compliance escalation policy. Be sure to cover all new lawyers as they join the legal department.

436 **Foreign lawyers.** Find outside counsel at each key foreign location and provide them with full background on the company's compliance and ethics program. This helps ensure they are qualified to help with local implementation of the program. They can also warn you of otherwise unanticipated pitfalls, such as local labor and privacy laws.

437 **Cost allocations.** Have the preventive compliance steps (e.g., training, policies, newsletters, etc.) absorbed as corporate overhead so business units are not required to pay directly for an ounce of prevention. But have the units pay the full costs of problems they create, e.g., investigations, penalties, etc.

438 **Sharing the experiences.** At the compliance committee level, review the experiences of each business unit and pass along what is learned from their successes and failures to all the units. (See Singer, "General Electric Company's True Confessions Ethics Video," *ethikos* 15 no. 2 (Sept./Oct. 2001): 5, 6.)

S. Documentation

It can be important for management of a compliance and ethics program, and also for convincing skeptical outsiders, to have the program documented. Here are some ideas related to documentation.

439 **Document everything.** Have a system for documenting all aspects of the compliance program effort. Assign someone specific responsibility to collect and retain all relevant program records.

440 **Training on privilege.** Provide training on the requirements for asserting privilege for all those involved in documenting the program.

441 **Audit the program files.** Conduct audits of the compliance program files, to ensure that all elements are covered adequately.

442 **Mock presentations.** Conduct mock presentations of the program using the documentation, to test its completeness and clarity.

443 **Presentation binder.** Have a binder containing the key documents relating to each element of the compliance and ethics program, and explaining where to find all additional documents associated with the program. Each risk area may also have its own binder.

444 **Indexing.** For all the compliance and ethics program documents in digital form, have a search or indexing system so that important documents can be located and recalled quickly and easily.

445 **Training records.** Retain records of the compliance training, including attendance logs, descriptions of the sessions, and copies of materials distributed. (See HHS, "OIG Compliance Program Guidance for Pharmaceutical Manufacturers," *Federal Register* 68 (May 5, 2003): 23,731, 23,740.)

446 **Disciplinary records.** Have records of compliance discipline that demonstrate seriousness and consistency, but reduce the risk of the records being used against the company. This might involve the use of summaries and other abbreviated records. (See Murphy, "Taking a Disciplined Approach to Discipline: Enforcing Compliance Standards," *ethikos* 13 no. 5 (Mar./Apr. 2000): 4, 11.)

T. Antitrust and fair competitive practices compliance

Every company that competes has antitrust and competition law exposure. Here are ideas for addressing this risk.

447 **DOJ's hidden video.** Use the U.S. Department of Justice's hidden video of the Lysine antitrust conspiracy in training sessions to illustrate dramatically what price fixing and market allocation are about.

448 **Intelligence gathering guidelines.** Provide a guideline of *dos* and *don'ts* for gathering competitive information, including useful tips on how to obtain such information legally and ethically.

449 **Trade association pocket card.** Provide a set of *dos* and *don'ts* on attending trade association meetings on a pocket-sized laminated card.

450 **Trade association programs.** Require or request any trade association in which your company participates to have its own, active compliance and ethics program.

451 **Limits on attending trade association meetings.** Place limits on who can attend trade association meetings, and require successful completion of antitrust training as a prerequisite. (See Sigler & Murphy, *Interactive Corporate Compliance: An Alternative to Regulatory Compulsion* (Westport, CT: Quorum Books, 1988): 91.)

452 **Timing of decisions.** Have a policy that bars price changes or similarly sensitive actions immediately after trade association meetings. (See Sigler & Murphy, *Interactive Corporate Compliance: An Alternative to Regulatory Compulsion* (Westport, CT: Quorum Books, 1988): 91.)

453 **Red flags list for auditors.** Develop a list of antitrust red flags and dangerous language to guide those conducting antitrust compliance audits. (See Kolasky, "Antitrust Compliance: The Government's Perspective," *ethikos* 16 no. 2 (Sept./Oct. 2002): 6, 13.)

454 **Antitrust FAQs.** Provide a set of FAQs or Q&As on antitrust basics, especially covering misconceptions, such as the erroneous belief that collusion will not be prosecuted against those in small markets or with small market shares.

455 **Antitrust *dos* and *don'ts*.** Give employees a very direct and practical set of antitrust *dos* and *don'ts*. (See Kolasky, "Antitrust Compliance: The Government's Perspective," *ethikos* 16 no. 2 (Sept./Oct. 2002): 6, 7.)

456 **OFT's guides.** Review the U.K. Office of Fair Trading's guides on competition law compliance for ideas on the compliance program in general, and particularly in the U.K. (See Murphy, "Compliance Guidance From the United Kingdom," *ethikos* 20 no. 5 (Mar./Apr. 2007): 5; *How Your Business Can Achieve Compliance*, (London: Office of Fair Trading, 2005), http://www.oft.gov.uk/shared_oft/business_leaflets/ca98_mini_guides/oft424.pdf.)

457 **Advance written approvals.** To prevent violations by rogue employees for discretionary matters involving competition — e.g., decisions on pricing, when not to bid or pursue particular business opportunities, and production levels — require advance written approval from headquarters, which could include review by an antitrust lawyer. (See Sigler & Murphy, *Interactive Corporate Compliance: An Alternative to Regulatory Compulsion* (Westport, CT: Quorum Books, 1988): 90.)

458 **Tracking communications.** It can be required that all phone communications and e-mail exchanges with competitors (or other key parties) be recorded and reviewed by legal. This may be viewed as extreme, and a step reserved for areas where there have been prior problems.

459   **Data analysis.** Certain competitive patterns may indicate collusive conduct, e.g., if there are only four competitors in a market and each one's sales are concentrated in particular geographic areas, or there is a distinct, non-random pattern of wins and losses on bidding. The company could develop a program for monitoring such data for any particular offices, as indicators of potential problem areas.

460   **Mandatory written reports.** Certain high-risk activities could require written reports from the participants to legal counsel/compliance officials, e.g., reports on all contacts with competitors, any competitors' communications through a customer or supplier, any decision not to pursue a customer or market, etc.

461   **Prohibit high-risk activities.** Employees could be barred from certain types of activity that may be legal but involve high antitrust risk, e.g., social contacts with competitors, e-mail contacts with competitors, accepting any correspondence without a return address, attendance at trade association meetings, etc. This may be viewed as extreme, and a step reserved for areas where there have been prior problems.

462   **Limit conference attendance.** Require prior authorization for attendance at industry conferences and social events attended by competitors. (See *United States v. Stolt-Nielsen SA*, Cr. No. 06-cr-466, Findings of Fact (E.D. Pa., Nov. 30, 2007): 32.)

463   **Antitrust handbook.** Issue an antitrust compliance handbook, spelling out what conduct is prohibited, what requires prior approval, and what are the consequences of violations. (See *United States v. Stolt-Nielsen SA*, Cr. No. 06-cr-466, Findings of Fact (E.D. Pa., Nov. 30, 2007): 19-21, 23, 28, 30-31.)

464 **Testing the training.** Test employees' knowledge of the company's competition policy and procedures, and of the antitrust law. (See Murphy, "Compliance Guidance From the United Kingdom," *ethikos* 20 no. 5 (Mar./Apr. 2007): 5, 6.)

465 **Knowledge contests.** Have a contest to see which sales team scores the highest on a challenging antitrust test. (See Murphy, "Testing Out," *ethikos* 21 no. 4 (Jan./Feb. 2008): 9, 11.)

466 **RP forms.** Require completion of an explanation form for off-list pricing, to cover Robinson-Patman compliance. (See Sigler & Murphy, *Interactive Corporate Compliance: An Alternative to Regulatory Compulsion* (Westport, CT: Quorum Books, 1988): 89.)

467 **Audit employees' understanding.** Audit key employees' understanding of the antitrust rules and their compliance with compliance program requirements. (See Roberts, "Antitrust Compliance Programs Under the Guidelines: Initial Observations From the Government's Viewpoint," *Corporate Conduct Quarterly* (now *ethikos*) 2 (Summer 1992): 1, 3.)

468 **10 rules.** Provide a certificate for those completing the antitrust training that lists on its face 10 rules or *dos* and *don't*s. (See Murphy, "Job Aides, Toys or 'Tchatchkas': Getting the Compliance Message to Employees," *ethikos* 14 no. 5 (Mar./Apr. 2001): 8, 9.)

469 **"No sale."** Provide a T-shirt or sweat shirt with a picture of a businessperson in jail and the slogan, "no sale is worth jail." (See Murphy, "Job Aides, Toys or 'Tchatchkas': Getting the Compliance Message to Employees," *ethikos* 14 no. 5 (Mar./Apr. 2001): 8, 11.)

U. FCPA/foreign corruption compliance

If a company does business outside its own borders it faces the risk of foreign bribery, a violation of the Foreign Corrupt Practices Act (FCPA) or similar statutes in other countries. Here are pointers on controlling this risk.

470 **Red flag lists.** Provide a list of corruption red flags to all those who are at risk for bribery opportunities. This list can include things like agents with no offices, and consultants requiring payment to third parties outside of the country.

471 **Due diligence list.** Provide a list of due diligence steps for those hiring third parties, such as agents and distributors in other countries.

472 **Compliance manual.** Provide a practical compliance manual for those doing work in other countries. This could include FAQ's, a red flags list, and guidance on conducting due diligence when retaining third parties.

473 **Scripts to say "no."** Develop scripts for employees working in foreign locations so they know what to say when approached for a bribe. (See Baldassano, "Train Employees on How to Say No to Demands for Bribes," *Prevention of Corporate Liability* 15 (Nov. 19, 2007): 152.)

474 **Performance standards.** Have a system for revising employees' performance standards if they have to miss business opportunities in order to refuse bribe requests. (See Baldassano, "Train Employees on How to Say No to Demands for Bribes," *Prevention of Corporate Liability* 15 (Nov. 19, 2007): 151, 152.)

475 **TI index.** Use the Transparency International list of most corrupt nations as a guide to prioritizing FCPA compliance efforts. (See "Chronikos," *ethikos* 16 no. 3 (Nov./Dec. 2002): 10.)

476 **Expense forms.** For international business, if your company permits facilitating payments, add a separate line to expense reports specifically to cover such payments. (See Singer, "Fluor Gets Behind PACI's Anti-Corruption Drive," *ethikos* 21 no. 3 (Nov./Dec. 2007): 14, 15.)

477 **No training, no travel.** Require completion of FCPA training before authorizing any employee for foreign travel. (See Murphy, "Reducing Foreign Corrupt Practices Act Risk: An Effective Self-Policing Program," *Corporate Conduct Quarterly* (now *ethikos*) 5 (1996): 28, 30.)

478 **Scholarship funds.** In an environment where professionals, such as doctors, cannot afford to attend conferences/seminars, and companies previously paid for them to attend, the industry members can establish a scholarship fund, not tied to any one company, to cover attendance costs. (See Singer, "Becton Dickinson's Ethics Troubleshooter," *ethikos* 20 no. 2 (Sept./Oct. 2006): 1, 3.)

479 **Controls on retaining agents.** Set strict limits on who can retain foreign agents, have a system of checks on such retentions, and require background checks. (See Murphy, "Reducing Foreign Corrupt Practices Act Risk: An Effective Self-Policing Program," *Corporate Conduct Quarterly* (now *ethikos*) 5 (1996): 28, 30.)

480 **Disclosures to government.** Consider disclosing to local governments the facts of any agency or consultant relationship. If the agent objects, this is a red flag. (See Murphy, "Reducing Foreign Corrupt Practices Act Risk: An Effective Self-Policing Program," *Corporate Conduct Quarterly* (now *ethikos*) 5 (1996): 28, 37.)

481 **Compliance presence.** In foreign locations, especially in high-risk locations, have designated compliance liaisons to champion the compliance and ethics message. (See Murphy, "Reducing Foreign Corrupt Practices Act Risk: An Effective Self-Policing Program," *Corporate Conduct Quarterly* (now *ethikos*) 5 (1996): 28, 30.)

482 **Gift lists.** In areas where it is customary to give gifts, have a list and/or supply of pre-approved gifts. These may have the company logo on them, to reduce their market value. (See Singer, "Becton Dickinson's Ethics Troubleshooter," *ethikos* 20 no. 2 (Sept./Oct. 2006): 1, 3.)

483 **Consultant interviews.** Personally interview foreign consultants and other reps as part of the pre-retention due diligence. (See Singer, "Titan Paid a Giant Price for FCPA Missteps," *ethikos* 19 no. 4 (Jan./Feb. 2006): 6, 7.)

484 **Check references.** Check references of consultants and other third parties in the pre-retention due diligence. (See Singer, "Titan Paid a Giant Price for FCPA Missteps," *ethikos* 19no. 4 (Jan./Feb. 2006): 6, 8.)

485 **Local laws.** Consider adding local counsel and local bribery laws to the FCPA presentation, to show that this is not just a U.S.-based issue. (See Murphy, "Reducing Foreign Corrupt Practices Act Risk: An Effective Self-Policing Program," *Corporate Conduct Quarterly* (now *ethikos*) 5 (1996): 28, 30.)

486 **Ask the government.** Talk with the government about what gifts, meals, travel, etc., are permissible in particular circumstances. (See Singer, "Raytheon's Gratuities and Gifts Policy Has Some Give," *ethikos* 15 no. 4 (Jan./Feb. 2002): 4, 5.)

487 **Gifts and gratuities grid.** Develop a matrix for different gifts and conflicts issues, based on different jurisdictions where the company does business. (See Singer, "Raytheon's Gratuities and Gifts Policy Has Some Give," *ethikos* 15 no. 4 (Jan./Feb. 2002): 4, 5-6.)

488 **Internal audit questionnaire.** Provide an FCPA questionnaire for internal audit to use as a standard part of all audits conducted in foreign locations. Internal audit simply records the answers and provides them online to counsel or the compliance office. (From Karen Wilson.)

V. Consumer protection, sales practices, and advertising compliance

If you deal with consumers, you have consumer-protection risk. Here are some ideas for handling this risk.

489 **Advertising review.** Require that all advertising receive prior sign-off by the law department. (See Murphy, "When Starting Your Compliance Program, Survey What's Already in Place—and in Practice," *ethikos* 16 no. 5 (Mar./Apr. 2003): 5, 6.)

490 **Advertising guide.** Provide a how-to advertising guide, covering rules and regulations, but also other useful information that will cause advertising people to use it frequently. This can also cover your company's trademark usage.

491 **Mystery shopping.** Include in a retail mystery-shopping program a requirement for observations and questions relating to consumer protection, such as pricing accuracy.

492 **Customer surveys.** Have an independent, outside firm conduct surveys of customers to test the effectiveness of sales supervisory controls. (See Jordan & Murphy, "Compliance Programs: What the Government Really Wants," *ACCA Docket* (July/Aug. 1996): 10, 26; *SEC v. Prudential Securities, Inc.,* CV93-2164 (D.D.C., Oct. 21, 1993).)

493 **Test calls.** Include test calls to your customer service sales and service staff. If you already do this to measure business performance, include compliance and ethics as part of the review. (From Dan Roach.)

W. Gifts and conflicts of interest compliance

Every company faces issues with gifts and potential conflicts of interest. This is an area where compliance and ethics programs can provide enormous help in surfacing and resolving issues. Here are some of the tools.

494 **Gifts to charities.** In circumstances where it is customary to give gifts, consider giving a gift to a charity in the other person's name. Be sure there is no quid quo pro, and in foreign locations, be sure this meets FCPA standards. (See Singer, "Becton Dickinson's Ethics Troubleshooter," *ethikos* 20 no. 2 (Sept./Oct. 2006): 1, 3.)

495 **Vet with executives.** Review drafts of standards for gifts and conflicts of interest with the senior managers. It is important to be sure managers are on board and can live with the new standards before they are set. (See Kaplan, Murphy & Swenson, "Are Conflicts of Interest Your Program's Achilles Heel?" *ethikos* 15 no. 2 (Sept./Oct. 2001): 1-2.)

496 **More ideas.** For more ideas and approaches on compliance and ethics efforts dealing with conflicts of interest, see Walker, *Conflicts of Interest in Business and the Professions: Law and Compliance* (Eagan, MN: Thomson/West; 2005 & Ann'l Supp.)

497 **Gift raffles.** When suppliers or other third parties give gifts, accept them on behalf of the company; later they might be raffled off to employees. (See Singer, "Becton Dickinson's Ethics Troubleshooter," *ethikos* 20 no. 2 (Sept./Oct. 2006): 1, 3.)

498 **Safe harbors.** Set safe harbor thresholds for gifts and entertainment so that employees know that expenditures below a certain amount do not require further scrutiny. Note, however, that certain types of gifts and entertainment (e.g., quid pro quos) are never allowed regardless of amount. (See Kaplan, Murphy & Swenson, "Are Conflicts of Interest Your Program's Achilles Heel?" *ethikos* 15 no. 2 (Sept./Oct. 2001): 1, 3.)

499 **Reporting thresholds.** Set reporting/review thresholds, so that certain types or amounts of gifts, entertainment and conflicts always have to be reported/reviewed by management. (See Kaplan, Murphy & Swenson, "Are Conflicts of Interest Your Program's Achilles Heel?" *ethikos* 15 no. 2 (Sept./Oct. 2001): 1, 3.)

500 **Know your customer.** Establish a "know your customer" rule, requiring sales people to find out about their customers' gifts and conflicts rules to avoid embarrassing violations. (See Kaplan, Murphy & Swenson, "Are Conflicts of Interest Your Program's Achilles Heel?" *ethikos* 15 no. 2 (Sept./Oct. 2001): 1, 10.)

501 **Team effort.** Involve supply chain management and the business development people in writing the gifts and conflicts-of-interest policy, so those who must live with it have input and buy in to the standards. (See Singer, "Raytheon's Gratuities and Gifts Policy Has Some Give," *ethikos* 15 no. 4 (Jan./Feb. 2002): 4.)

Bibliography of Sources

BOOKS

Kaplan, Jeffrey M. & Murphy, Joseph E., *Compliance Programs and the Corporate Sentencing Guidelines* (Eagan, MN: Thomson/West; 1993 & Ann'l Supp).

Murphy, Joseph E., & Leet, Joshua H., *Building a Career in Compliance and Ethics* (Minneapolis: Society of Corporate Compliance and Ethics; 2007).

Murphy, Joseph E., & Leet, Joshua H., *Working for Integrity: Finding the Perfect Job in the Rapidly-Growing Compliance and Ethics Field* (Minneapolis: Society of Corporate Compliance and Ethics; 2006).

Nelson, Bob, *1001 Ways to Reward Employees* (New York: Workman Publishing Co.; 1994).

Sigler, Jay A., & Murphy, Joseph E., *Corporate Lawbreaking and Interactive Compliance* (Westport, CT: Quorum Books, 1991).

Sigler, Jay A., & Murphy, Joseph E., *Interactive Corporate Compliance: An Alternative to Regulatory Compulsion* (Westport, CT: Quorum Books; 1988).

Walker, Rebecca S., *Conflicts of Interest in Business and the Professions: Law and Compliance* (Eagan, MN: Thomson/West; 2005 & Ann'l Supp).

ARTICLES

Baldassano, Valli, "Train Employees on How to Say No to Demands for Bribes," *Prevention of Corporate Liability* 15 (Nov. 19, 2007): 152.

Bavuso, Margaret, & Murphy, Joseph E., "The Compliance Investigation: How to Conduct Effective Interviews," *Prevention of Corporate Liability Current Report* 11 (July 21, 2003): 72.

Baylson, Michael M., "Getting the Demons Into Heaven: A Good Corporate Compliance Program," *Corporate Conduct Quarterly* (now *ethikos*) 2 (Winter 1992): 33.

Beil, Mary Ann Bowman, "How Memorial Health Measures the Ethics Performance of its Senior Managers," 18 *ethikos* 18 no. 4 (Jan./Feb 2005): 8.

Berg, Jim, "Ethics and the Inclusion of the Virtual Workforce," *ethikos* 14 no. 2 (Sept./Oct. 2000): 7.

Bevilacqua, Francesca Chiara, "Corporate Compliance Programs Under Italian Law," 20 *ethikos* 20 no. 2 (Nov./Dec.2006): 1.

Boehme, Donna C., "How BP Communicates Integrity: Creative Engagement to Win Hearts and Minds," *ethikos* 19 no. 5 (Mar./Apr. 2006): 1.

Boehme, Donna C., & Murphy, Joseph E., "No Place to Hide: Early Lessons from the Siemens Case," *ethikos* 21 no. 3 (Nov./Dec. 2007): 10.

Crawford, David B., "Using Peer Reviews to Assess Your Compliance Program," *ethikos* 18 no. 5 (Mar./Apr. 2005): 12.

Daly, Frank, "Ethics Programs and the Changes in the Boardroom," *ethikos* 14 no. 2 (Sept./Oct. 2000): 4.

Di Santo, Carrie J., & Hengesbaugh, Brian, "U.S. Helplines Raise EU Privacy Concerns," *ethikos* 19 no. 2 (Sept./Oct. 2005): 1.

Frankcom, Mark, "Ssh, Ssh Don't Tell Me!" *ethikos* 21 no. 4 (Jan./Feb. 2008): 12.

Goldfarb, Jeff, Cass, Dwight, & Sanati, Cyrus, "Too Many Days on the Job," *Wall Street Journal* (Jan. 29, 2008): C14.

Hoffman, W. Michael, Driscoll, Dawn-Marie, & Rowe, Mark, "Effective Ethics Education of the Board," *ethikos* 18 no. 4 (Jan./Feb. 2005): 1.

Hoffman, W. Michael, & Rowe, Mark, "The Ethics Officer and the Board: Partners for Effective Ethical Governance," *ethikos* 21 no. 2 (Sept./Oct. 2007): 8.

"How United Technologies' Board Meets its Compliance Obligations," *ethikos* 11 no. 1(July/Aug. 1997): 4.

"In Search of Disciplinary Consistency," *ethikos* 14 no. 4 (Jan./Feb. 2001): 12.

"Investigation, Termination—and the Aftermath," *ethikos* 11 no. 4 (Jan./Feb. 1998): 5.

Jordan, Kirk S., & Murphy, Joseph E., "Are You Buying Trouble? Ignoring Target Company's Compliance Efforts Could Be Folly," *Prevention of Corporate Liability Current Report* 5 (Oct. 20, 1997): 12.

Jordan, Kirk S., & Murphy, Joseph E., "Compliance Programs: What the Government Really Wants," *ACCA Docket* 10 (July/Aug. 1996).

Kaplan, Jeffrey M., "Compliance Programs for Smaller Companies," *ethikos* 21 no. 4 (Jan./Feb. 2008): 6.

Kaplan, Jeffrey M., "Five Questions for a Risk Analysis," *ethikos* 14 no. 6 (May/June 2001): 4.

Kaplan, Jeffrey M., "Post-Enron Expectations: Directors, Investigations and Independence of Process," *ethikos* 17 no. 1 (July/Aug. 2003): 1.

Kaplan, Jeffrey M., "Risk-Based Compliance Program Management," *ethikos* 19 no. 5 (Mar./Apr. 2006): 7.

Kaplan, Jeffrey M., "Sundstrand's 'Responsible Executive' Program," *Corporate Conduct Quarterly* (now *ethikos*) 4 (1996): 33.

Kaplan, Jeffrey M., "The Board's Role in Ethics Programs: A Global Study," *ethikos* 17 no. 5 (Mar./Apr. 2004): 1.

Kaplan, Jeffrey M., "The Boss's New Job: Ensuring Compliance Program Effectiveness," *ethikos* 18 no. 6 (May/June, 2005): 1.

Kaplan, Jeffrey M., "The Ethics Officer Association's Risk Assessment Survey," *ethikos* 18 no. 3 (Nov./Dec. 2004): 1.

Kaplan, Jeffrey M., "The Tone at the Middle," *ethikos* 20 no. 2 (Sept./Oct. 2006): 5.

Kaplan, Jeffrey M., "Thinking Inside the Box: Risk Analysis in Three Dimensions," ethikos 14 no. 2 (Sept./Oct. 2000): 1.

Kaplan, Jeffrey M., Murphy, Joseph E., & Swenson, Winthrop M., "Are Conflicts of Interest Your Program's Achilles Heel?" *ethikos* 15 no. 2 (Sept./Oct. 2001): 1.

Kolasky, William J., "Antitrust Compliance: The Government's Perspective," *ethikos* 16 no. 2 (Sept./Oct. 2002): 6.

Leet, Joshua H., "A New Compliance Certification Program," *ethikos* 20 no. 4 (Jan/Feb 2007): 15.

Lipps, Linda, "Regional Business Ethics Roundtables: The Greater Houston Experience," *ethikos* 21 no. 2 (Sept./Oct. 2007): 11.

Lipson, Barry J., "A Survey on the Ins and Outs of Antitrust Compliance," *Antitrust Law Journal* 51 (1982): 517.

Martens, Lori Tansey, & Crowell, Amber, "Whistleblowing: A Global Perspective (Part II)," *ethikos* 16 no. 1 (July/Aug. 2002): 9.

Mintz, James, & Frost, Edward, "Transparency in Due-Diligence Background Checking: Setting a Standard," *ethikos* 18 no. 6 (May/June 2005): 5.

Murphy, Joseph E., "Compliance Guidance From the United Kingdom," *ethikos* 20 no. 5 (Mar./Apr. 2007): 5.

Murphy, Joseph E., "Compliance Officers: One Part Ombudsman, Two Parts Watchdog," *National Law Journal* (Dec. 14, 1992): S2.

Murphy, Joseph E., "Enhancing the Compliance Officer's Authority: Preparing an Employment Contract," *ethikos* 11 no. 6 (May/June 1998): 5.

Murphy, Joseph E., "Facility Compliance Coordinator Position Could Help Ensure That Compliance Program Reaches the Field," *Prevention of Corporate Liability Current Report* 4 (Dec. 16, 1996): 12.

Murphy, Joseph E., "Hotlines, an Overview," *Corporate Conduct Quarterly* (now ethikos) 4 (1995): 7.

Murphy, Joseph E., "How the CEO Can Make the Difference in Compliance and Ethics," *ethikos* 20 no. 6 (May/June 2007): 9.

Murphy, Joseph E., "How to Respond to Compliance Failures," *ALI-ABA Course Materials Journal* 16 (June 1992): 7.

Murphy, Joseph E., "Industry Practices Groups: Why and How," *ethikos* 20 no. 1 (July/Aug 2006): 12.

Murphy, Joseph E., "Internet's Speed, Efficiency Has Raised the Bar for Employee Compliance Training," *Prevention of Corporate Liability Current Report* 8 (Apr. 17, 2000): 32.

Murphy, Joseph E., "I've Been Waiting for You to Call," *ethikos* 19 no. 6 (May/June 2006): 15.

Murphy, Joseph E., "Job Aides, Toys or 'Tchatchkas:' Getting the Compliance Message to Employees," *ethikos* 14 no. 5 (Mar./Apr. 2001): 8.

Murphy, Joseph E., "Lost Words of the Sentencing Guidelines," *ethikos* 16 no. 3 (Nov./Dec. 2002): 5.

Murphy, Joseph E., "'Mandavolent' Compliance," *ethikos* 19 no. 2 (Sept./Oct. 2005): 8.

Murphy, Joseph E., "New Ideas for Managing Business Ethics and Legal Compliance," *The Journal of Commerce & Finance* (Villanova University) 8 (Fall 1991): 11.

Murphy, Joseph E., "Protections for Compliance People," in Murphy, Joseph E. and Leet, Joshua H., *Working for Integrity: Finding the Perfect Job in the Rapidly-Growing Compliance and Ethics Field* (Minneapolis: Society of Corporate Compliance and Ethics, 2006): 397-416.

Murphy, Joseph E., "Questions to Ask About an In-House Compliance and Ethics Job Offer," *ethikos* 18 no. 3 (Nov./Dec. 2004): 7.

Murphy, Joseph E., "Reducing Foreign Corrupt Practices Act Risk: An Effective Self-Policing Program," *Corporate Conduct Quarterly* (now *ethikos*) 5 (1996): 28.

Murphy, Joseph E., "Surviving the Antitrust Compliance Audit," *Antitrust Law Journal* 59 (1991): 953.

Murphy, Joseph E., "Taking a Disciplined Approach to Discipline: Enforcing Compliance Standards," *ethikos* 13 no. 5 (Mar./Apr. 2000): 4.

Murphy, Joseph E., "Testing Out," *ethikos* 21 no. 4 (Jan./Feb. 2008): 9.

Murphy, Joseph E., "The Measurement Challenge (Part I): Introducing the Deep Dive," *ethikos* 17 no. 6 (May/June 2004): 7; "The Measurement Challenge (Part II): Implementing the 'Deep Dive,'" *ethikos* 18 no. 1 (July/Aug 2004): 11; "The Measurement Challenge (Part III): Results from the 'Deep Dive,'" *ethikos* 18 no. 2 (Sept./Oct. 2004): 11.

Murphy, Joseph E., "Training 'in a Practical Manner,'" 6 *Corporate Conduct Quarterly* (now *ethikos*) 6 (1998): 2.

Murphy, Joseph E., "When Starting Your Compliance Program, Survey What's Already in Place—and in Practice," *ethikos* 16 (Mar./Apr. 2003): 5.

Murphy, Joseph E., & McCollum, Douglass J., "Communicating 'in a Practical Manner:' Bell Atlantic's Report on Integrity," *Corporate Conduct Quarterly* (now *ethikos*) 4 (1996): 59.

Murphy,. Joseph E., & Roach, Daniel R., "Compliance Officer on Board: What Your Audit Committee is Missing," *ethikos* 20 no. 3 (Nov/Dec 2006): 12.

Murphy, Joseph E., & Swenson, Winthrop M., "20 Questions to Ask About Your Code of Conduct," *ethikos* 17 no. 1 (July/Aug. 2003): 7.

Murphy, Joseph E., & Vigale, Christopher, "The Role of Incentives in Compliance Programs," *ethikos* 18 no. 6 (May/June 2005): 8.

Muse, Dennis, "Hotlines Must Adapt to an Ever-Changing Global Environment," *ethikos* 20 no. 4 (Jan../Feb. 2007): 11.

Nortz, Jim, "Unread, Codes of Conduct Become Dangerous Dust Collectors," *ethikos* 19 no. 4 (Jan./Feb. 2006): 9.

Parmenter, Deanna, "Eight Reasons Smaller Companies Should Have Compliance Programs," *ethikos* 18 no. 2 (Sept./Oct. 2004): 9.

Petry, Edward S., "Assessing Corporate Culture," *ethikos* 18 no. 5 (Mar./Apr. 2005): 1.

Petry, Edward S., "Assessing Corporate Culture: Part II," *ethikos* 19 no. 1 (July/Aug. 2005): 10.

Petry, Edward S., "EOA Survey: Companies Seeking to Integrate Ethics Through the Whole Organization," *ethikos* 15 no. 1 (July/Aug. 2001): 1.

Pompa, Victor, & Petry, Edward S., "More Companies Are Looking at Ethics in the 'Extended Organization,'" *ethikos* 12 no. 5 (Mar./Apr. 1999): 7.

Redmond, Arlene, & Williams, Randy, "The Organizational Ombuds: Complementing the Ethics office," *ethikos* 17 no. 2 (Sept./Oct. 2003): 10.

Roach, Robert F., & Davis, Mara, "Establishing a Culture of Ethics and Integrity in Government," *ethikos* 21 no. 2 (Sept./Oct. 2007): 1.

Roberts, Neil E., "Antitrust Compliance Programs Under the Guidelines: Initial Observations From the Government's Viewpoint," *Corporate Conduct Quarterly* (now *ethikos*) 2 (Summer 1992): 1.

"Sara Lee Corporation Relies On its Business Practices Officers Overseas," *ethikos* 11 no. 3 (Nov./Dec. 1997): 4.

Scarpino, Steve, "NCR Corporation's Four-fold Ethics & Compliance Model," *ethikos* 20 no. 1 (July/Aug. 2006): 7.

Sears, Brian, "Lights! Camera! Action! Lockheed Martin's Ethics Film Festival," *ethikos* 17 no. 4 (Jan/Feb 2004): 8.

Sharpe, Brian, "Checking Your Compliance Program's Performance—By the Numbers," *ethikos* 16 no. 6 (May/June 2003): 10.

Sharpe, Brian, "The Value of a Complaints System in Effective Legal Compliance Systems," *ethikos* 18 no. 3 (Nov/Dec 2004): 11.

Sherwood, Emily L., "Screening Job Applicants for Ethics: Can it be Done?" *ethikos* 20 no. 3 (Nov./Dec. 2006): 8.

Sherwood, Emily L., "The Evolving Position of Ethics Officer," *ethikos* 20 no. 1 (July/Aug. 2006): 10.

Sherwood, Emily L., "The Exit Interview: A Final Compliance Check," *ethikos* 18 no. 6 (May/June 2005): 13.

Singer, Andrew W., "AEP's Ethics Interviews Are 'About the Passion of the People,'" *ethikos* 13 no. 6 (May/June 2000): 1.

Singer, Andrew W., "Alliance-Bernstein Invests in New Ombuds office, *ethikos* 19 no. 6 (May/June 2006): 12.

Singer, Andrew W., "An Ethics Officer of Olympian Proportions," *ethikos* 18 no. 2 (Sept./Oct. 2004): 6.

Singer, Andrew W., "At Bellsouth, the Main Ethics Website is the Internal One," *ethikos* 14 no. 4 (Jan./Feb. 2001): 8.

Singer, Andrew W., "At Tenet Healthcare: Linking Ethics to Compensation," *ethikos* 14 no. 4 (Jan./Feb. 2001): 4.

Singer, Andrew W., "Audits Reduce Compliance Risk at United Technologies," *ethikos* 14 no. 5 (Mar./Apr. 2001): 12.

Singer, Andrew W., "Aventis' Helpline: Translating from the Urdu (et al.)," *ethikos* 17 no. 3 (Nov./Dec. 2003): 4.

Singer, Andrew W., "Becton Dickinson's Ethics Troubleshooter," *ethikos* 20 no. 2 (Sept./Oct. 2006): 1.

Singer, Andrew W., "Boeing Company's Ethics Improvements Take Flight," *ethikos* 20 no. 1 (July/Aug. 2006): 5.

Singer, Andrew W., "Born of strife, DTE's heterogeneous ethics council advises," *ethikos* 15 no. 6 (May/June 2002): 9.

Singer, Andrew W., "Bracing for Deregulation, AEP Boosts Ethics Training," *ethikos* 11 no. 1 (July/Aug. 1997): 1.

Singer, Andrew W., "Caremark and Tenet's Prescription: 'Live' Ethics Training," *ethikos* 19 no. 1 (July/Aug. 2005): 17.

Singer, Andrew W., "Caterpillar's Code Revisions: Reinforcing the 'High' Way," *ethikos* 20 no. 2 (Sept./Oct. 2006): 8.

Singer, Andrew W., "Coming This Season to KNTV: Marathon's Business Code of Conduct," *ethikos* 17 no. 3 (Nov./Dec. 2003): 9.

Singer, Andrew W., "Coors Brewing Company's Ethics Code Training," *ethikos* 16 no. 2 (Sept./Oct. 2002): 4.

Singer, Andrew W., "Creating an Open, Non-Retaliatory Workplace," *ethikos* 19 no. 5 (Mar./Apr. 2006): 4.

Singer, Andrew W., "Developing *Effective* Helplines: Shell Oil and Lubrizol," *ethikos* 19 no. 2 (Sept./Oct. 2005): 5.

Singer, Andrew W., "Do You Know Me? I'm the American Express Ombudsperson….," *ethikos* 19 no. 2 (Sept./Oct. 2005): 12.

Singer, Andrew W., "Ethics Training at Lockheed Martin Takes a Tabloid Turn," *ethikos* 15 no. 1 (July/Aug. 2001): 8.

Singer, Andrew W., "Exelon Excels at Reaching Out," *ethikos* 16 no. 6 (May/June 2003): 7.

Singer, Andrew W., "Fannie Mae Rates Managers On Integrity and Honesty," *ethikos* 17 no. 1 (July/Aug. 2003): 4.

Singer, Andrew W., "Fluor Gets Behind PACI's Anti-Corruption Drive," *ethikos* 21 no. 3 (Nov./Dec. 2007): 14.

Singer, Andrew W., "General Electric Company's True Confessions Ethics Video," *ethikos* 15 no. 2 (Sept./Oct. 2001): 5.

Singer, Andrew W., "Granite Construction Adds 'Land Mines' to its Antitrust Compliance Training," *ethikos* 18 no. 6 (May/June 2005): 15.

Singer, Andrew W., "Honda's Ethics Training Shifts to a Higher Gear," *ethikos* 13 no. 4 (Jan./Feb. 2000): 6.

Singer, Andrew W., "How Dow Chemical Centralized its Investigations Process," *ethikos* 19 no. 1 (July/Aug. 2005): 1.

Singer, Andrew W., "How the World Bank Revised its Code of Conduct," *ethikos* 15 no. 3 (Nov./Dec. 2001): 4.

Singer, Andrew W., "How TRW's Legal and Ethics Compliance is Reviewed Annually," *ethikos* 15 no. 2 (Sept./Oct. 2001): 7.

Singer, Andrew W., "How Xerox Weaves Ethics Into the Internal Audit Process," *ethikos* 20 no. 5 (Mar./Apr. 2007): 11.

Singer, Andrew W., "Is a Company Ethical? Just Ask the Competition," *ethikos* 16 no. 3 (Nov./Dec. 2002): 1.

Singer, Andrew W., "KPMG Seeks to Propel Ethics to the 'Ends of the Tentacles,'" *ethikos* 21 no. 3 (Nov./Dec. 2007): 4.

Singer, Andrew W., "Learning from the Salt Lake City Olympics Scandal," *ethikos* 14 no. 5 (Mar./Apr. 2001): 1.

Singer, Andrew W., "Marsh's Business Reforms: Much Ground Covered in Little Time," *ethikos* 19 no. 6 (May/June 2006): 1.

Singer, Andrew W., "Motorola's Ethics Renewal Process," *ethikos* 12 no. 1 (July/Aug. 1998): 4.

Singer, Andrew W., "Needed from Bertelsmann's Ethics & Compliance Officer: A 'Diplomatic Effort,'" *ethikos* 17 no. 2 (Sept./Oct. 2003): 7.

Singer, Andrew W., "Ombuds office Helps Coca-Cola Bottler Avoid Explosions," *ethikos* 19 no. 3 (Nov/Dec 2005): 11.

Singer, Andrew W., "Packaging an Ethics Code: Altria Learns That One Size Doesn't Fit All," *ethikos* 18 no. 4 (Jan/Feb 2005): 4.

Singer, Andrew W., "Raytheon's Gratuities and Gifts Policy Has Some Give," *ethikos* 15 no. 4 (Jan./Feb. 2002): 4.

Singer, Andrew W., "Shell Oil Company 'Energizes' its Ethics Commitment," *ethikos* 16 no. 3 (Nov./Dec. 2002): 8.

Singer, Andrew W., "Southern Company Sets Sights on Self-Monitoring," *ethikos* 14 no. 2 (Sept./Oct. 2000): 12.

Singer, Andrew W., "Sun Microsystems Sends Managers to Fiduciary Boot Camp," *ethikos* 16 no. 5 (Mar./April 2003): 8.

Singer, Andrew W., "TAP Pharma Isn't Afraid to Show 'A Little Levity,'" *ethikos* 19 no. 5 (Mar./Apr. 2006): 16.

Singer, Andrew W., "The 1950s: Eisenhower, the Yankees, Senator McCarthy and an Ethics Committee," *ethikos* 15 no. 2 (Sept./Oct. 2001): 11.

Singer, Andrew W., "The Timken Company Assesses its Worldwide Compliance Conference," 11 *ethikos* 11 no. 5 (Mar./Apr. 1998): 5.

Singer, Andrew W., "Titan Paid a Giant Price for FCPA Missteps," *ethikos* 19 no. 4 (Jan./Feb. 2006): 6.

Singer, Andrew W., "Tying Ethics to Evaluations at Nationwide Insurance Company," *ethikos* 21 no. 5 (Mar./Apr. 2008).

Singer, Andrew W., "UPS Translates and Transports an Ethics Code Overseas," *ethikos* 14 no. 5 (May/June 2001): 1.

Singer, Andrew W., "Values is the Bedrock Upon Which Suez Builds," *ethikos* 15 no. 3 (Nov./Dec. 2001): 11.

"The Conference Board Benchmarks Ethics and Compliance Programs," *ethikos* 20 no. 3 (Nov./Dec. 2006): 14.

Walker, Rebecca S., "Extending Compliance Requirements to Suppliers and Other Third Parties," *ethikos* 19 no. 6 (May/June 2006): 5.

Walker, Rebecca S., "New Code Requirements: Preliminary Answers to Some Emerging Questions," *ethikos* 18 no. 2 (Sept./Oct. 2004): 1.

Walker, Rebecca S., "The NYSE Report: Analyzing its Impact On Corporate Compliance Programs," *ethikos* 16 no. 1 (July/Aug. 2002): 1.

"Walking the Talk," *ethikos* 16 no. 5 (Mar./April 2003): 12.

Webb, "Ottenberg's: A Recipe for Rewarding Safety: Bakery's Incentive Program Cuts Costs, Improves Productivity," *Washington Post* (Feb. 19, 1990): F11.

Zinn, Herbert, "*ComplianceGrams*: A Case Study in Communicating and Teaching Compliance," *Corporate Conduct Quarterly* (now *ethikos*) 4 (1995): 1.

ONLINE RESOURCES

Building Incentives in Your Compliance & Ethics Program, SCCE white paper, http://www.corporatecompliance.org/Content/NavigationMenu/Resources/IssuesAnswers/DRAFTwhitepaper-BuildingIncentivesCompliance_WOappdx.pdf.

ethikos Web site: http://www.ethikosjournal.com/.

Society of Corporate Compliance and Ethics (SCCE) Web site: www.corporatecompliance.org.

CASES

In re Caremark International Inc. Derivative Litigation, 698 A.2d 959 (Del. Ch. 1996).

In re Grumman Corp., settlement agreement (E.D.N.Y., Nov. 23, 1993).

SEC v. Prudential Securities, Inc., CV93-2164 (D.D.C., Oct. 21, 1993).

United States v. C.R. Bard Inc., CV93-10276-T, plea agreement (D. Mass; Oct. 14, 1993).

United States v. Stolt-Nielsen SA, Cr. No. 06-cr-466, Findings of Fact (E.D. Pa., Nov. 30, 2007).

GOVERNMENT POLICIES/STATEMENTS

HHS, "OIG Compliance Program Guidance for Pharmaceutical Manufacturers," 68 *Fed. Reg.* 68 (May 5, 2003): 23,731.

Office of Inspector General of the U.S. Department of Health and Human Services and the American Health Lawyers Association, *Corporate Responsibility and Corporate Compliance: A Resource for Health Care Boards of Directors* (Office of Inspector General of the U.S. Department of Health and Human Services, 2003), http://oig.hhs.gov/fraud/docs/complianceguidance/040203CorpResp RsceGuide.pdf.

U.S. Sentencing Guidelines, Section 8B2.1.